Directory of Irish Archives

FOURTH EDITION

Edited by

Seamus Helferty and Raymond Refaussé

FOUR COURTS PRESS

This book was set
in 10.5 on 12 Times Roman.
Published in Ireland by
FOUR COURTS PRESS LTD
7 Malpas Street, Dublin 8, Ireland
e-mail: info@four-courts-press.ie
http:\\www.four-courts-press.ie
and in North America by
FOUR COURTS PRESS
c/o ISBS, 920 N.E. 58th Street, Suite 300, Portland, OR 97213.

First edition, 1988
Second edition, 1993
Third edition, 1999
Fourth edition, 2003

A catalogue record for this title
is available from the British Library.

ISBN 1–85182–778–1 hbk
ISBN 1–85182–779–x pbk

Printed in Great Britain by
Creative Print and Design (Wales) Ebbw Vale.

Contents

Introduction

It has been the custom with successive editions of this directory to use the introduction as an opportunity to review developments in the general condition of Irish archives. The period between the first (1988) and second (1993) editions was marked by the implementation of the *National Archives Act 1986*. Statutory regulation of public archives and initial steps to provide adequate accommodation and staffing had an undoubted effect in raising public consciousness. Together with a more leisured and informed research clientele and one, it must be said, with ever higher expectations, the general effect was a greater vitality in Irish archives.

This was witnessed by the rise in the number of entries from the first to the second edition from 155 to 224. This increase was due not entirely to extra diligence on the part of the editors but was a genuine reflection of the allocation of additional resources and the development of a greater willingness on the part of record keepers to make proper disposition for their collections and to allow consultation. It was significant that the largest single category of institution in that second edition was church, and particularly congregational, archives. The end of the century saw much rationalisation in this sector. The closure of religious houses and consequent consolidation was a contributory factor to even greater centralisation of archival resources in Dublin.

The counterbalance to this trend was the emergence of a number of local authority archives services, the impetus for which was provided by Section 65 of the *Local Government Act 1994*. This placed a statutory responsibility upon local authorities to manage and preserve their archives and to make them accessible to the public. It is fair comment that the response of the local authorities to their new obligations has been neither consistent nor thorough. Many authorities have taken their responsibilities very seriously, employing professional archivists and securing or upgrading accommodation; but this has not been the universal response. The preservation of archives on a scale appropriate to a modern local authority requires the employment of a professional archivist. More than 50 per cent of Irish local authorities have failed to do this. Seasonal shortages of qualified professionals cannot be blamed for a failure to establish and maintain a proper archives service and those local authorities unwilling to allocate the necessary resources cannot expect to attract or keep qualified and experienced staff.

If archival developments in more recent years have lacked impact this is at least partly due to the difficulty of sustaining the rate of progress that characterised the late 1980s and 1990s; and the fact that the attention of legislators has turned in other directions in the context of recordkeeping, most obviously demonstrated by the *Freedom of Information Act 1997*. It is arguable, however, that the emergence of a climate of openness and accountability was made possible only by the earlier establishment of an orderly regime in our public archives. One noteworthy recent development in this sector has been the long-awaited release for consultation of the records of the Bureau of Military History 1913–21, now in the curatorship of the Military Archives. The release of this immensely significant collection not only provides a wealth of source material for the history of the independence movement, but also confounds the sceptics who doubted the resolve of those responsible to take a necessary and overdue decision.

The compilation of this edition took place in incremental stages during the first five months of 2003. Existing entries were updated as a first step. This usually took the form of changing contact details and adding e-mail and website addresses. The increased prevalence of these indicates an inevitable trend towards use of a website as the primary means of promoting the holdings of an institution; and of e-mail as the preferred route of contact. E-mail addresses are an area where the editors have been forced to compromise their long-standing preference to cite positions and job titles as contacts rather than the personal names of office holders. So many e-mail addresses are personal that it would have been impossible to maintain this preference. Where possible, the *Major collections* section of each entry was amended also to reflect development since 1999.

Potential new entries were then approached and sent a copy of a standard questionnaire. If it is possible to isolate any specific category of institution to which additions or amendments have been made, it is the local authority archives services mentioned earlier. These take the form of completely new entries; as well as major alterations to existing entries to indicate the emergence of an archives service from collections already held by another service of the local authority, usually the library.

It is worthwhile restating some of the caveats that have accompanied all editions: that the editors have consciously omitted categories of institution, such as businesses and trades unions covered by other surveys and publications; that, as with all directories of this sort, the quality of the finished article is dependent in large part on the quality of the information supplied or elicited; and that, irrespective of opening hours indicated, it is always worthwhile contacting an institution in advance of a visit to confirm the existence and availability of relevant sources and ascertain the existence of any additional requirements for access.

With regard to contact details, a word should be said about area codes which have been included with telephone numbers. The area codes given for both jurisdictions are internal ones and adjustments should be made for cross-border calls. When phoning a Northern Ireland institution from the Republic of Ireland the first three digits should be changed from 028 to 048. Calls from Northern Ireland to the Republic are international calls and the initial 0 should be changed to 00 353.

The publication of another edition of this directory brings to mind the origin of the series in a suggestion by the late Dr Philomena Connolly that a short guide to Irish repositories be prepared to inform delegates, mostly from the United Kingdom, attending the annual conference of the Society of Archivists in Dublin in 1984. It was with this intention that a small working party of the then Irish Region of the Society began to gather data on the rather more restricted range of archives services that existed in the wilderness years predating the *National Archives Act 1986*. That the extent of those services proved too extensive for the confines of a short guide does nothing to minimise the significance of Dr Connolly's seminal concept. Her untimely death in June 2002 has deprived the Irish archival community in general and the National Archives in particular of an outstanding archivist.

If successive editions of this publication have appeared under the names of just two members of that original working group, this should not mask the contribution that the membership of the Society of Archivists, Ireland and Irish archivists in general continue to make to its usefulness and modest success. The editors would like to thank all those curators whose cooperation in providing information allows the directory to lay some claim to being a reliable and up-to-date *entrée* for those seeking information on the holdings of Irish archives and procedures for their consultation; their colleagues in the Representative Church Body Library and University College Dublin Archives Department; and Michael Adams, Martin Fanning and Ronan Gallagher of Four Courts Press for their sustained interest in this project.

May 2003

1   AIB Group

Address   Bankcentre
                       Ballsbridge
                       Dublin 4

Telephone   (01) 641 4487

Enquiries to   Group Archivist

Opening hours By postal enquiry from researchers providing suitable
and facilities   references; facilities by arrangement

Major collections

La Touche & Co. (1693–1870): small collection of account books and ledgers.

Provincial Bank of Ireland (1825–1966): board minutes, circulars from head offices in London and Dublin, personnel registers.

Royal Bank of Ireland (1836–1966): board minutes, annual accounts, personnel registers.

Munster Bank Ltd (1864–85): small collection of banking records.

Munster and Leinster Bank Ltd (1885–1966): board minutes, head office circulars, personnel records.

2   Airfield Trust

Address   Airfield
                       Upper Kilmacud Road
                       Dublin 14

Telephone   (01) 298 4301

Fax   (01) 296 2832

Website   www.airfield.ie

Enquiries to   The Archivist

Opening hours By arrangement
and facilities

Major collections

Private family papers of the Overend family (Dublin), 19th century.

3   Alexandra College

Address	Milltown Dublin 6
Telephone	(01) 497 7571
Fax	(01) 497 4873
E-mail	alexcold@iol.ie
Website address	www.iol.ie/~alexcold/
Enquiries to	The Archivist/Librarian
Opening hours and facilities	9.00–4.00, Mon–Fri; appointment necessary; initial letter to the College Principal outlining research project; photocopying
Guides	Anne V. O'Connor & Susan M. Parkes, *Gladly learn and gladly teach* (1984) is a history of the College with a bibliography of sources.

Major collections

College Council minutes, 1866–1930, and extracts from minutes, 1930–66.
Lady Principals' reports, 1930–45.
Committee of Education minute books, 1866–1911.
Alexandra School Committee of Education minutes, 1887–1939.
Alexandra College Registers of Proficiency and Progress, 1866–72, 1882–1914.
Alexandra College daily roll book, 1879–81.
Lady Superintendent's notes, 1876–86.
Finance Committee account book, 1882–1926.
Collection of College publications including the prospectus, 1866–76; Alexandra College Magazine, 1893–98; Alexandra College, Dublin, Jubilee Record, 1866–1916; and College calendars, 1879–1901.

4   All Hallows College

Address	Grace Park Road Drumcondra Dublin 9
Telephone	(01) 837 3745

Fax	(01) 837 7642
E-mail	archives@allhallows.ie
Website	www.allhallows.ie
Enquiries to	The College Archivist
Opening hours and facilities	By appointment

Major collections

Correspondence between Catholic bishops and priests and the College of All Hallows, 1842–; correspondence is from Britain, USA, Australia, Canada, New Zealand, India, Mauritius, West Indies, Argentina and South Africa.

The early correspondence, 1842–77, has been microfilmed and is available in many overseas state and national libraries.

5   Allen Library

Address	Edmund Rice House North Richmond Street Dublin 1
Telephone	(01) 855 1077
Fax	(01) 855 5243
E-mail	allenlib@connect.ie
Website	www.allenlibrary.com
Enquiries to	The Curator/Librarian/Archivist
Opening hours and facilities	10.00–4.00, Mon–Fri; by appointment only; photocopying; photographic database

Major collections

Material relating to the Congregation of Christian Brothers including O'Connell Schools' roll books, 1831–1949 (excluding 1841–54, 1859–80, 1892, 1898–1903); records of scholarship holders, 1953–65; administration records, 1915–22; school account books, 1930–35, 1938–39; choir lists, 1931–32; class lists, 1938–41; examination results, 1879–1929;

Intermediate Examination results, 1919–25; First Communion lists, 1858–87, 1860–1901; St Laurence O'Toole School attendance books, 1921–53; school register, 1916–67; admission register, 1876–1916; pupil information register, 1926–35; papers of individual members of the Congregation of Christian Brothers.

Material relating to the history of modern Ireland actively acquired by Br William Palladius Allen, mainly 1916–22, including papers and photographs of prominent political figures including Eamonn Ceannt, P.H. Pearse (mainly concerning St Enda's School), Dr Kathleen Lynn, Madeline ffrench Mullen and Alice Milligan.

The collection also contains material preceding 1916, outside the main focus of the collection, relating to Irish local and social history; and 30,000 publications, including a considerable collection of pamphlets and journals, on the local, national, educational and ecclesiastical history of Ireland, with a section on the history and development of the Congregation of Christian Brothers.

6   Apothecaries Hall

Address   95 Merrion Square
                Dublin 2

Telephone   (01) 676 2147

Enquiries to   Apothecaries Hall

Opening hours and facilities   By appointment

Guides   M. Clark and R. Refaussé (eds), *Directory of historic Dublin guilds* (Dublin, 1993)

Major collections

Minutes of the Guild of Apothecaries (Guild of St Luke the Evangelist), 1747–1820.

Records of the Company of Apothecaries Hall: minutes, accounts, correspondence, lists of apprentices, assistants and certificate holders, 1791–; signatures to oaths of office, 1795–; lists of licentiates, 1859–; examination records, 1897–; attendance books, 1899–.

7   Ardagh & Clonmacnoise Diocesan Archives

Address	Bishop's House Longford
Telephone	(043) 46432
Fax	(043) 46833
E-mail	archives@stmelscollege.ie
Enquiries to	The Archivist
Opening hours and facilities	By appointment.

Major collections

Ardagh Diocesan Archives contain considerable collections of papers which formed the correspondence of bishops during the 19th century. The papers begin *c.*1820, being noticeably incomplete up to 1853. The episcopate of George Conroy is represented by a small collection. The largest collection is that of Bartholomew Woodlock, 1879–95. There is very little material either extant or available after 1895.

8   Armagh County Museum

Address	The Mall East Armagh BT61 9BE
Telephone	(02837) 523070
Fax	(02837) 522631
E-mail	catherine.mccullough.um@nics.gov.uk/ greer.ramsey.um@nics.gov.uk
Website	www.magni.org
Enquiries to	The Curator
Opening hours and facilities	10.00–5.00, Mon–Fri

Major collections

T.G.F. Paterson collection: historical and genealogical manuscripts relating primarily to family pedigrees and local history with particular reference to County Armagh.

George Russell (Æ) (1867–1935): small collection of papers including poems, letters and drawings.

Blacker daybooks: handwritten accounts by Col. William Blacker (1775–1855) of contemporary events including the battle of the Diamond, 1795, and of sermons preached by him.

Estate papers including records of the Charlemont estate, 18th–19th centuries: leases, account books, maps and surveys.

Copies of records relating to County Armagh including: hearth money rolls, 1664; muster rolls, 1630; poll book, 1753; census of Armagh City, 1770; First Armagh Presbyterian Church registers, 1727–9, 1796–1809; abstracts from the rentals of the archbishops of Armagh, 1615–1746; Manor of Armagh tenants, 1714; abstracts of depositions, 1641.

9   Armagh Observatory

Address	College Hill Armagh BT61 9DG
Telephone	(02837) 522928
Fax	(02837) 527174
E-mail	meb@arm.ac.uk (Director) jmf@arm.ac.uk (Librarian)
Websites	star.arm.ac.uk www.rascal.ac.uk
Enquiries to	The Director or Librarian
Opening hours and facilities	9.30–4.30, Mon–Fri; photocopying
Guides	J. Butler & M. Hoskin, 'The archives of Armagh Observatory', *Journal for the History of Astronomy* 18 (1987) lists archival material up to 1916 and is available on the www. J.A. Bennett, *Church, state and astronomy in Ireland – 200 Years of Armagh Observatory* (Armagh Observatory, 1990). J. McFarland, 'The rare and antiquarian book collection of Armagh Observatory', *Irish Astronomical Journal* 33 (1990).

Major collections
Directors and astronomers papers: J.A. Hamilton (1748–1815), T.R. Robinson (1793–1882), J.L.E. Dreyer (1852–1926), E.J. Öpik (1893–1985) and E.M. Lindsay (1937–1974).

Correspondence relating to the Boyden Observatory, South Africa.

Astronomical observations of the positions of stars, planets and nebulae, 1782–1914.

Meteorological records from Armagh, 1785–.

Astronomical photographs taken with the Armagh Schmidt telescope, 1950–*c*.70, and the Armagh–Dunsink–Harvard telescope, 1950–74.

Estate papers relating to Derrynaught, Tullynure and Carlingford, 1790–1910, deposited with the Public Record Office of Northern Ireland (q.v.).

10   [Armagh] Public Library

Address	Abbey Street Armagh BT61 7DY
Telephone	(02837) 523142
Fax	(02837) 524177
E-mail	ArmRobLib@aol.com
Enquiries to	The Keeper
Opening hours and facilities	10.00–1.00, 2.00–4.00, Mon–Fri; at other times by appointment; photocopying, photography
Guides	*Catalogue of manuscripts in the Public Library of Armagh* (1928)

Major collections

Papers of Anthony Dopping, bishop of Meath (1682–97) relating to the diocese of Meath.

Correspondence of Lord John George Beresford, archbishop of Armagh (1822–62).

Papers of William Reeves, bishop of Down (1882–96) relating to Irish church history from the 5th to the 19th century.

Records of 17th and 18th century episcopal visitations.

Copies of Armagh primatial registers, 1362–.

11   Bank of Ireland Group

Address	Head Office, A5
	Lower Baggot Street
	Dublin 2
Telephone	(01) 661 3920
Fax	(01) 661 5705
E-mail	Derville.Murphy@boimail.com
Website	www.bankofireland.ie
Enquiries to	Derville Murphy, Group Architect
Opening hours and facilities	Postal enquiry

Major collections

Archives of all major departments and offices of the Bank: Court of Directors including Court of Directors' Transactions or Minute Books, 1783–; Secretary's Office including Secretary's correspondence; Accountant General's Office including Account Books; Audit Office including reports on branches; Architect's Office including plans and photographs of branches; Branch Banks Office including memoranda from Head Office to branches and branch records; Law Agent's Office and Staff Office.

Extensive archives of the Hibernian Bank (1825–1958) and the National Bank (1834–1966) which merged with the Bank of Ireland.

12   Belfast Central Library

Address	Royal Avenue
	Belfast BTI IEA
Telephone	(02890) 509150
Enquiries to	The Librarian, Belfast, Ulster & Irish Studies
E-mail	infobelb@ni–libraries.net
Website	www.belb.org.uk
Opening hours and facilities	By appointment; photocopying

Major collections

F.J. Bigger (1863–1926): 40,000 items. F.J. Bigger wrote and researched
    on local historical topics. He was editor of the *Ulster Journal of
    Archaeology*, but his interests were wide ranging and included all aspects
    of Belfast history, the United Irishmen, later nationalist movements and
    the revival of the Irish language. The collection includes his own corre-
    spondence and correspondence collected by him.

J.S. Crone (1858–1945): 10,000 items. J.S. Crone was president of the Irish
    Literary Society in London, founder and first editor of the *Irish Book
    Lover* and author of the *Concise dictionary of Irish biography*. The col-
    lection reflects these interests.

A.S. Moore (1870–1961): 1,000 items. Cuttings, pamphlets, indexes and
    compilations on local history, with special emphasis on industry.

A. Riddell (1874–1958): 5,000 items. Cuttings, indexes and compilations
    on social history and local biography.

Bryson and Macadam Collection: 44 manuscript volumes, late 18th and
    early 19th centuries, recording Ulster legends, poems and songs in the
    Irish language.

Literary collections including manuscripts, correspondence and diaries of
    Amanda McKittrick Ros, Forrest Reid, Sam Thompson, Lynn Doyle, St
    John Irvine and Alexander Irvine.

13   Belfast Harbour Commissioners

Address	Corporation Square Belfast BT1 3AL
Telephone	(02890) 554422
Fax	(02890) 554411
E-mail	info@belfast-harbour.co.uk
Website	www.belfast-harbour.co.uk
Enquiries to	Corporate Affairs Executive
Opening hours and facilities	By appointment only

Major collections

Records of various bodies, relating to Belfast and its port, 1600–.

14   Birr Castle

Address	Birr County Offaly
Telephone	(0509) 20023
Fax	(0509) 20425
Website	www.birrcastleireland.org
Enquiries to	The Secretary The Estate Office Ross Row
Opening hours and facilities	By appointment; access to archives is restricted to those enrolled as Friends of Birr Castle Demesne; initial enquiries by post or fax only; photocopying

Major collections

Correspondence and related papers of successive Earls of Rosse, 1595–; including correspondence and biographical material relating to Henry Flood, 1765–*c.*1820, friend and political mentor of Sir Laurence Parsons, 2nd earl, whose own papers, 1775–1841, include correspondence, political material, poetry, the history and genealogy of the Parsons family, as well as documents relating to the 1798 Rebellion, the Union, and his term as joint postmaster for Ireland, 1809–31.

Correspondence of the 3rd and 4th earls, 1840–1909, particularly with other astronomers concerning Birr and other observatories; journals containing astronomical observations, and drafts for articles and speeches on astronomy; glass plate collection of Mary, countess of Rosse, a pioneer photographer, 1854–60; letters and papers relating to Sir Charles Parsons, younger brother of the 4th earl and inventor of the steam turbine engine.

Non-scientific correspondence of the 3rd to 7th earls, 1840–1991, including correspondence of the 3rd earl as president of the Royal Society, 1848–54, and of the 3rd and 4th earls as chancellors of Dublin University.

Extensive collection of papers and correspondence of the 6th earl and countess of Rosse, 1918–79.

Estate office archives, 1604–1979, including maps, plans and drawings; leases and leasebooks; rentals, rent and other accounts; Irish Land Commission papers, 1874–1970; agents' correspondence, 1879–1965; and material relating to the families and Yorkshire estates of the wives of the 3rd, 4th and 5th earls, the Wilmer Field family of Heaton Hall, Bradford; the Hawke family including papers of Admiral Sir Edward Hawke, 1st Lord Hawke and First Lord of the Admiralty, 1766–71; and the Lister Kaye family of Denby Grange, near Wakefield.

15   Bolton Library

Address	John Street Cashel County Tipperary
Telephone	(062) 61944
Fax	(062) 61944
E-mail	boltonlibrary@oceanfree.net
Website	www.heritagetowns.com
Enquiries to	The Custodian
Opening hours and facilities	By appointment
Guides	*Catalogue of the Cashel Diocesan Library* (Boston, 1973)

Major collections

Church of Ireland archives: parish records from the Cashel, Dundrum, Tipperary and Aherlow areas, 17th century–; Cashel Cathedral records, late 18th century–.

Miscellaneous ecclesiastical and secular manuscripts (deeds and legal documents, maps and plans, diaries, research notes and writings), and photographs, mainly 17th–19th century but including two 13th-century and one 14th-century English liturgical manuscripts.

16   Carlow Central Library

Address	Tullow Street Carlow County Carlow
Telephone	(0503) 70094
Fax	(0503) 40548
E-mail	library@carlowcoco.ie
Website	www.carlow.ie
Enquiries to	The County Librarian

Major collections

The Local Studies Collection includes the Jackson, Bruen, and Tyndall collections; and the Baggot Papers, Burton Papers and Vigors Papers as well as extensive collections of local newspapers, copies of cartographic, census, and valuation records, and folklore of local interest.

17   Cashel & Emly Diocesan Archives

Address	Archbishop's House Thurles County Tipperary
Telephone	(0504) 21512
Fax	(0504) 22680
E-mail	office@cashel–emly.ie
Website	www.cashel–emly.ie
Enquiries to	The Archivist, St Patrick's College, Thurles, County Tipperary (q.v.)
Opening hours and facilities	By appointment, but originals are made available only in exceptional circumstances. Researchers are advised to consult the microfilm copies of the documents in the National Library, Kildare Street, Dublin. Permission is required to consult the material but is readily given to bona fide researchers. Alternatively, facilities are provided to read the microfilm copies of the documents in St Patrick's College, Thurles; photocopying
Guides	Calendars of the papers in Cashel Diocesan Archives are provided both in the National Library and in Thurles. Some of these have been published by Revd Mark Tierney in *Collectanae Hibernica* 9, 13, 16–20. Other material from the archives has been published by Revd Mark Tierney in *Collectanae Hibernica* 11 and 12 and by Revd Christopher O'Dwyer in *Archivium Hibernicum* 33 and 34.

Major collections

Cashel Diocesan Archives contain large collections of the papers of the

Archbishops of Cashel since the early 18th century. These papers are an important source for the history of the archdiocese of Cashel as well as containing much material of national interest. The archives contain only a small number of items which are pre-18th century. The material is catalogued under the names of the various archbishops of Cashel since the 18th century. At present the archives are accessible up to the death of Archbishop Croke in 1903.

The archives also contain the Skehan Index of Clergy of the archdiocese of Cashel and Emly.

Further material belonging to the Cashel Diocesan Archives is in St Patrick's College, Thurles, where it may be consulted by arrangement. This material, the Skehan and Fogarty Papers, consists of two large collections of handwritten historical, biographical and genealogical notes relevant to the ecclesiastical and civil history of the archdiocese of Cashel and surrounding area since the 18th century. The material is being computerised and listed and copies of the lists will shortly be deposited in the Tipperary Joint Libraries, Thurles, County Tipperary (q.v.).

18   Castle Matrix

Address	Rathkeale County Limerick
Telephone	(069) 64284/086 837 1737
Fax	(069) 63242
Enquiries to	The Director
Opening hours and facilities	By appointment

Major collections

Castle Matrix was the headquarters of the International Institute of Military History and of the Heraldry Society of Ireland until 1991. The archives include: papers relating to the Irish 'Wild Geese' in the service of France and Spain, including a contemporary map of the battle of Fontenoy and the order of battle 1745, 1690–1820; heraldic manuscripts including the 572 Ordinary of Arms of Robert Cooke (Clarencieux King of Arms) comprising over 10,000 coats of arms; and documents relating to the Paris Commune, 1871.

Military archives including the papers of the rocket scientist Dr Clarence Hickman and papers relating to the air war in Europe and the Pacific, 1939–.

19 Cavan County Library

Address	Farnham Street Cavan
Telephone	(049) 433 1799
Fax	(049) 437 1832
E-mail	cavancountylibrary@tinet.ie cavancountylibrary@eircom.net
Enquiries to	The County Librarian
Opening hours and facilities	11.00–1.00, 2.00–5.00, 6.00–8.30, Mon, Thur; 11.00–5.00, Tue, Wed; 11.00–1.00, 2.00–5.00, Fri; photocopying
Guides	Sources for Cavan Local History, *Breifne*, 1977–8. Guide to County Cavan Local Studies Department

Major collections

Copy charter of the town of Belturbet by George III; copy charter of the town of Cavan by James II, 28 February 1688.

Famham Estate papers.

Account book and rent roll for the Saunderson Estate, Belturbet, 1768–71.

Maps of drainage and navigation of Ballinamore/Ballyconnell, passing from Lough Erne to the Shannon, 1846.

Ordnance Survey maps, 1835; Mornington Estate maps, 1853; Cavan–Leitrim Railway maps.

Griffith Valuation maps, 1848–64.

Collection of legal documents, leases, rentals, wills, for County Cavan, 18th and 19th century.

Barron Papers.

Registers, account and fee books, inspectors reports from Bailieboro Model School, 1860s–1900s.

Board of Guardian minute books, 1839–1921.

Rural District Council minute books, 1899–1925.

Newspaper cuttings from national and provincial newspapers on the '2nd' or 'New Reformation' in Cavan, with lists of those who conformed to the established church, 1824–6. Speeches and posters relating to the 1826 election in Cavan (microfilm).

Diary of Randal McCollum, Presbyterian minister, Shercock, County Cavan, describing social conditions, 1861–71.

Photographs: Eason collection; Valentine collection; miscellaneous pho-

tographs and postcards relating to County Cavan, 20th century; railway
photographic collection; Farnham family album.
Dean Richardson's *Leabhar na Nornaightheadh Comhchoithienn* [Book of
Common Prayer], *Caitecism na hEaglaise* and *Short history of the attempts.*

20   **Chester Beatty Library**

Address	Dublin Castle
	Dublin 2
Telephone	(01) 407 0750
Fax	(01) 407 0760
E-mail	info@cbl.ie
Website	www.cbl.ie
Enquiries to	The Librarian and Director
Opening hours and facilities	Exhibition galleries and main areas
	10.00–5.00, Mon–Fri, May–Sept
	10.00–5.00, Tue–Fri, Oct–April
	11.00–5.00, Sat; 1.00–5.00 Sun, all year
	Reference Library
	10.00–1.00, 2.15–5.00, by appointment
	photocopying; photography; microfilming; photocopying of manuscripts is not allowed
Guides	A list of publications available for sale can be obtained from the Library or viewed on the website.

Major collections
The collection was the private library of Sir Alfred Chester Beatty
(1875–1968), bequeathed on his death to the Irish people. The manuscript
collection dates from several thousand years BC to the 20th century.
Manuscript holdings include:
Cuneiform clay tablets from the Berens collection.
Egyptian papyri: hieratic papyri containing love poems from *c.*1160 BC and
a finely preserved Book of the Dead of the Lady Neskons.
Greek papyri include those collected by Wilfred Merton and the famous
Biblical Papyri, eleven codices in all, 2nd–4th century AD.
Among the Coptic papyri are the texts of the lost books of the Manichaean
faith and several biblical texts. There are small collections of Hebrew,
Samaritan, Coptic and Syriac vellum manuscripts, mostly biblical.

Among the Syriac is a 5th-century commentary on the Diatessaron by St Ephraim.

There is a small but significant collection of Western manuscripts, including a 12th-century Walsingham Bible and several fine Books of Hours. The Slavonic manuscripts, also primarily biblical, are notable for their quality and illumination.

There are over 3,000 Arabic manuscripts in the collection covering every branch of religious and secular literature. The collection of Qurans includes a large number of early examples, including a 9th-century example written in gold on blue vellum and a unique Quran written at Bagdad in 1001 by Ibn al–Bawwab, a celebrated calligrapher. The Persian manuscripts cover the whole range of painting, calligraphy and book arts and include a fine 14th-century Shah–Namah.

The Indian section has many finely illustrated manuscripts in the Mughal style, including a chronicle of Akbar the Great. There are several Jain, Nepalese, Tamil, Kanarese and Sinhalese manuscripts.

The Burmese, Siamese, Tibetan and Mongolian collections number c.350 items and there are more than 40 Batak manuscripts from Sumatra, dealing mainly with magical subjects. The Chinese collection contains more than 170 hand-painted scrolls and albums, and 14 imperial jade books. In the Japanese collection there are c.100 scrolls and albums.

The Library also holds Chester Beatty's correspondence relating to the formation of the collection and the establishment of the Library, c.1910–68. Administrative records of the Library, 1968–.

21 Church of Ireland College of Education Archives

Address	Upper Rathmines Road Dublin 6
Telephone	(01) 497 0033
Fax	(01) 497 1932
E-mail	library@cice.ie
Enquiries to	The Librarian
Opening hours and facilities	By appointment. Normally materials can only be made available during academic term time. Please write for details and an application form; photocopying and photography may be permitted by special arrangement and in special circumstances

Major collections

Kildare Place Society collection: central administrative and financial records of the society; general, committee, parliamentary, publishing and inspectors' correspondence; correspondence between the Society and its schools; educational effects.

Church of Ireland Training College collection: records of the College, 1884–, and some earlier records of the Church Education Society training institution. (Certain classes and ages of documents are closed to researchers).

Other manuscript collections: Disestablishment correspondence, 1860s; Protestant Defence Association correspondence; Kildare Place Ex-Students Association in Northern Ireland collection, 1936–79.

Older printed books and textbooks: copies of textbooks and chapbooks published by the Kildare Place Society in the early 19th century, including those published in tablet or chart form, and a wide range of later 19th- and early 20th-century Irish textbooks.

22   Clare County Council

Address	New Road Ennis County Clare
Telephone	(065) 682 1616
Fax	(065) 682 0882
Website	www.clare.ie/
Enquiries to	The Archivist
Opening hours and facilities	By appointment

Major collections

Poor Law records of County Clare, 1850–1922
Clare County Council minute books, 1899–1968.
Minute books of the Board of Health and Public Assistance, 1921–42.
Finance Committee minute books, 1906–38.
Agenda books, 1946–68.
Manager's Orders, 1942–66.
Personnel records, 1945–68.
Planning files, 1961–.
Records of Our Lady's Mental Hospital, Ennis, 1868–1970.

Rural District Council minute books, 1898–1925.
Registers of electors, 1935–1970.

23 Clare County Library Local Studies Centre

Address	The Manse Harmony Row Ennis County Clare
Telephone	(065) 684 6271
Fax	(065) 684 2462
E-mail	mailbox@clarelibrary.ie
Website	www.clarelibrary.ie
Enquiries to	The Local Studies Librarian
Opening hours and facilities	10.00–1.00, 2.00–5.30, Mon; 10.00–1.00, 2.00–5.00, Tue–Fri; 10.00–2.00, Sat (except bank holiday weekends) photocopying, microfilm and fiche readers

Major collections
Grand Jury Presentments, 1854–1900; minute book of the Borough of Ennis, 1699–1810; maps.

24 Clogher Diocesan Archives

Address	Bishop's House Monaghan
Telephone	(047) 81019
Fax	(047) 84773
E-mail	cloghdiocoffmon@eircom.net
Enquiries to	The Archivist
Opening hours and facilities	11.00–1.00, Mon–Wed; photocopying

Guides
Guides   Microfilm and catalogue in Public Record Office of Northern Ireland (q.v.)

Major collections
Papers of James Donnelly, bishop of Clogher (1864–93).
Baptismal and marriage records for some parishes of the diocese to 1880.

25   Clogher Diocesan Archives [Church of Ireland]

Address	St Macartan's Cathedral Clogher County Tyrone BT76 0AD
Telephone	(02885) 548235
Enquiries to	The Dean or Mr J. Johnston, Secretary, Friends of Clogher Cathedral
Opening hours and facilities	By appointment

Major collections
Clogher diocesan records: visitations, rural deans' reports, maps, 18th–20th century.
Clogher chapter lease book, 18th–19th century.
Clogher Corporation book, 1783.

26   Clonalis House

Address	Castlerea County Roscommon
Telephone	(0907) 20014
E-mail	Clonalis@iol.ie
Enquiries to	The owner
Opening hours and facilities	By appointment
Guides	Gareth W. and J.E. Dunleavy (comps), *The O'Conor*

papers: a descriptive catalogue and surname register of the materials in Clonalis House (1977)

Major collections
Major collection of *c.*100,000 manuscripts, 16th century–, including the works of Charles O'Conor of Belanagare.

27   Clonfert Diocesan Archives

Address	St Brendan's
	Coorheen
	Loughrea
	County Galway
Telephone	(091) 841560
E-mail	clonfert@iol.ie
Fax	(091) 841818
Enquiries to	The Bishop of Clonfert
Opening hours and facilities	By appointment

Major collections
Title deeds and legal documents concerning diocesan property, 1793–.
Visitation books, conference and synod books, registers of clergy.
Correspondence and papers of individual bishops, including letters to and from Rome, pastoral letters, and material concerning general diocesan administration. These papers date from the 1830s but little survives from before the 1880s.

28   Clongowes Wood College

Address	Naas
	County Kildare
Telephone	(045) 868202
Fax	(045) 861042
E-mail	reception@clongowes.net
	mdoyle@clongowes.net

Website	www.clongowes.com
Enquiries to	The Rector/Archivist
Opening hours and facilities	Enquiries by post, telephone, e-mail or fax

Major collections
Complete register of pupils, parents or guardians, with addresses and fees, May 1814–.
Incomplete series of Journals of Prefects of Studies and of House Journals; academical exercises, mainly 1818–65; Rules for Masters and Rules for Pupils, with revised editions of both; registers of the Sodality of Our Lady and other pious organisations; minutes of the Social Study Club, 1913–25.
The Clongownian, annual, 1895–.

29   Cloyne Diocesan Archives

Address	Cloyne Diocesan Office Cobh County Cork
Telephone	(021) 481 1430
Fax	(021) 481 1026
E-mail	cloyne@indigo.ie
Enquiries to	The Archivist
Opening hours and facilities	Postal and telephone enquiries only

Major collections
Papers of bishops of the diocese.

30   Communist Party of Ireland

Address	43 East Essex Street Temple Bar Dublin 2
Telephone	(01) 671 1943

Fax	(01) 671 1943
E-mail	cpi@indigo.ie
Website	www.communistpartyofireland.ie
Enquiries to	The National Chairperson
Opening hours and facilities	By appointment

Major collections
Miscellaneous collections of newspapers, leaflets, journals, photographs and posters relating to the Communist Party of Ireland and its international relations over 70 years.
Materials dealing with working life since 1913 in Dublin, Belfast and Cork.
Materials on the Irish involvement in the Spanish Civil War, 1936–9.
Large collection of materials relating to strikes and working class and small farmer struggles.

31   Companies Registration Office

Address	Parnell House 14 Parnell Square Dublin 1
Telephone	(01) 804 5200
Fax	(01) 804 5222
E-mail	info@cro.ie
Website	www.cro.ie
Enquiries to	The Information Unit
Opening hours and facilities	10.00–1.00, 2.15–4.30, Mon–Fri; company searches and photocopying

Major collections
Files relating to *c.*160,000 Irish companies and 3,000 external companies dating from the 1890s.

32   Contemporary Music Centre Ireland

Address	19 Fishamble Street Temple Bar Dublin 8
Telephone	(01) 673 1922
Fax	(01) 648 9100
E-mail	info@cmc.ie
Website address	www.cmc.ie
Enquiries to	The Music Librarian
Opening hours and facilities	10.00–5.00, Mon–Fri
Guides	Information leaflet; information pack; newsletter *New Music News*; directory, *Irish Composers*

Major collections

Specialist collection of music by modern Irish composers. Includes music scores, sound archive and reference library relating to the compositions of Irish classical composers of the 20th and 21st centuries.

33   Córas Iompair Éireann

Address	Heuston Station Dublin 8
Enquiries to	The Secretarial Services Manager
Opening hours and facilities	Initial postal enquiry; subsequently by appointment; access is usually granted only to doctoral students; photocopying

Major collections

Minute books and committee minute books of the main constituent companies of CIÉ, 1840s–.

34   Cork Archives Institute

Address	Christ Church South Main Street Cork
Telephone	(021) 427 7809/492 8800
Fax	(021) 427 4668
E-mail	cai@indigo.ie
Website address	www.corkcity.ie/facilities
Enquiries to	The Archivist
Opening hours and facilities	10.00–1.00; 2.30–5.00 Tue–Fri; by appointment; closed Mon; photocopying; photography
Guides	Introductory leaflet; annual accessions lists. Ann Barry, 'Sources for labour history in the Cork Archives Institute', *Saothar* 10 (1984). Marita Foster, 'Hurley emigrant letters', *Irish Roots* 3 (1992). Patricia McCarthy, 'Maritime Records in Cork Archives Institute', *Irish Archives* 2, no. 1 (1992); 'Sources for the study of the Great Famine held at the Cork Archives Institute', *Journal of the Cork Historical & Archaeological Society* 102 (1997); 'The archives of local government in the Cork Archives Institute', *Irish Archives* 3, no. 2 (1996). *The Poor Law Records of County Cork,* Cork Archives Institute (1995). *Descriptive list of the papers of Liam Ó Buachalla*, Cork Archives Institute (1994). *Descriptive list of the Seamus Fitzgerald Papers* Cork Archives Institute (1999). Brian McGee, 'Sources for labour history at the Cork Archives Institute', *Saothar* 25 (2000).

Major collections

Archives of local authorities including Cork Corporation/Cork City Council, Cork County Council, Youghal Town (1906–65), Poor Law Union Boards of Guardians, rural district councils, town commissioners, urban district councils, Cork Board of Public Health, vocational educational committees.

Business records including Beamish & Crawford Brewery, Cork Distillers, Cork Butter Market, R. & H. Hall Corn Merchants, Sunbeam & Wolsey Textiles, Lunham Meats, B. & I. Line/Cork Steam Ship Company, Ogilvy & Moore Provisioners, Hickey & Byrne Printers.

Personal papers including Richard Dowden, Liam de Roiste, Seamus

Fitzgerald, J.J. Walshe, Barry M. Egan, Liam Ó Buachalla, Geraldine Cummins, Siobhán Lankford.

Landed estate records including Colthurst, Blarney; Newenham, Coolmore; Courtenay, Midleton; Coppinger, Ballyvolane and Carrigtwohill; Cooper Penrose, Cork; the earl of Bandon; Lord Doneraile.

Records of trades unions, clubs, societies, religious groups and schools including Cork Workers' Council, Cork Coopers' Society, Cork Typographical Union, Cork Plumbers' Union, Cork Presbyterian Congregation at Princes Street, Skiddy's Almshouse, Cork Grafton Club, Cork District Model School, Cork Sick Poor Society and Cork Theatre.

35   Port of Cork Company

Address	Harbour Office Custom House Street Cork
Telephone	(021) 427 3125
Fax	(021) 427 6484
E-mail	info@portofcork.ie
Website	www.portofcork.ie
Enquiries to	The Secretary
Opening hours and facilities	By appointment; photocopying

Major collections

Records of the Cork Harbour Commissioners who became defunct in March 1997; minutes of board meetings, 1814–; registers of arrivals and sailings, 1912–; Board members' attendance books, 1913–; registers of conveyances, 1836–1927; bye–laws, 1822–; accounts, 1871–; pilotage licences, 1924–.

36   Cork Public Museum

Address	Fitzgerald Park Mardyke Cork

Telephone	(021) 4270 679
Fax	(021) 4270 931
E-mail	museum@corkcity.ie
Enquiries to	The Curator
Opening hours and facilities	11.00–1.00, 2.15–5.00, Mon–Fri; by appointment; photocopying

Major collections
A large collection of documents and photographs, 1900–22, including the
MacCurtáin and MacSwiney papers.

37   Crawford Municipal Art Gallery

Address	Emmet Place Cork
Telephone	(021) 4273 377
Fax	(021) 480 5043
E-mail	crawfordgallery@eircom.net
Website	www.crawfordartgallery.com
Enquiries to	The Gallery Secretary
Opening hours and facilities	10.00–5.00, Mon–Sat; no admission after 4.45; photography
Guides	Information leaflets on request

Major collections
Material from the Cork School of Art library, dating from the mid–19th century, including many large portfolios on architecture and the decorative
arts. Material relating generally to art in Cork in the 19th century. Minute
books of the Technical Instruction Committee (later the Vocational
Education Committee) and incomplete student registers, 19th–20th centuries. Diaries relating to the Gibson family, early 19th century; John
Hogan architectural sketchbook, *c.*1830; 19th-century continental lace
and lace patterns.

38   De La Salle Brothers

Address   Castletown
Portlaoise
County Laois

Telephone   (0502) 32359

Enquiries to   The Archivist

Opening hours   Postal enquiry only;
and facilities   photocopying

Major collections
Material relating to the history of the congregation in Ireland.

39   Derry City Council
Heritage & Museum Service

Address   Harbour Museum
Harbour Square
Derry BT48 6AF

Telephone   (02871) 377331

Fax   (02871) 377633

E-mail   bernadette.walsh@derrycity.gov.uk
museums@derrycity.gov.uk

Website   www.derrycity.gov.uk

Enquiries to   The City Archivist

Opening hours   10.00–1.00, 2.00–4.30, Mon–Fri; by appointment;
and facilities   photocopying

Major collections
Archives of Derry City Council and its predecessor, Londonderry
Corporation, including minute books, 1673–1969; correspondence files
and letter books, 1849–1969; legal documents, 1679–1969; Rural District
Council minute books, 1908–69; architectural drawings, 1870–1969;
maps, 1830–1970; First World War War Memorial Registers; photographs
relating mainly to civic events and members of the Corporation.

Private collections: textiles collections from Tillie & Henderson's Shirt Factory and the City Factory, 1819–1965; railway collections from the Londonderry & Lough Swilly Railway Company, Great Northern Railway Company, Strabane & Letterkenny Railway Company, Buncrana & Carndonagh Light Railway Company, 1880–1920; theatre societies and local amateur dramatics groups; Gwyn's Charitable Institution, 1829–1945; Prior's Chemist, 1898–1947; A.A. Watt & Company Ltd, 1830–88; Derry Trades Council, 1964–92; Northern Ireland Civil Rights Association, 1969–75; Bridget Bond, 1970–6; Kathleen Coyle, 1923–52; Jack Scoltock, 1990–96;

40   Derry Diocesan Archive

Address   9 Steelstown Road
Derry BT48 8EU

Telephone   (02871) 359809

Fax   (02871) 359809

E-mail   Edward.Daly@btinternet.ie

Enquiries to   The Archivist

Opening hours and facilities   By appointment; photocopying

Major collections
Records of the diocese, 1939–.

41   Discalced Carmelites (Irish Province)

Address   St Teresa's Church
Clarendon Street
Dublin 2

Telephone   (01) 671 8466

Fax   (01) 671 8462

Enquiries to   The Provincial Secretary

Opening hours and facilities   Postal or telephone enquiry

Major collections

Material relating to the history of the Carmelite Community at Worm-
woodgate Chapel, 1707–57, Stephen Street Chapel, 1757–97, and
Clarendon Street Church, 1797–.

History of the various foundations made from Clarendon Street to elsewhere
in Ireland and overseas.

42   Dominican Provincial Archives

Address	St Mary's Priory
	Tallaght
	Dublin 24
Telephone	(01) 404 8100
Enquiries to	The Provincial Archivist
Opening hours	By appointment or by postal enquiry;
and facilities	photocopying

Major collections

Correspondence and papers of Dominican superiors and individuals,
1820–1922.

Collections of notes on Irish Dominican history by several historians of the
Order.

Account books of many Irish convents.

Archives of the Dominican College of Lisbon.

Newscuttings, sermons and publications of members of the Province.

Chapter legislation, 1720–.

Books of reception and profession.

43   Congregation of Dominican Sisters Cabra

Address	5 Westfield Road
	Harold's Cross
	Dublin 6W
Telephone	(01) 405 5570/5571
Fax	(01) 405 5682

E-mail	dhorganop@iolfree.ie
Website	www.cabraop.org
Enquiries to	The Congregation Archivist
Opening hours and facilities	By appointment; photocopying, scanning

Major collections

Material concerning the growth and activities of the congregation, 1644–, with special emphasis on the period, 1719–. Includes relations internal to the Dominican Order, with ecclesiastical authorities and other congregations; relating to the Sisters' involvement with all levels of education, primary, secondary, third level and ecumenical; and other pastoral ministeries undertaken by the Sisters in Ireland, South Africa, Portugal, Louisiana, Argentina, Brazil and Bolivia.

44   Donegal County Archives

Address	Donegal County Council Three Rivers Centre Lifford County Donegal
Telephone	(074) 917 2490
Fax	(074) 914 1367
E-mail	nbrennan@donegalcoco.ie
Website	www.donegal.ie
Enquiries to	The Archivist
Opening hours and facilities	By appointment; photocopying
Guides	Regularly updated *Overview of listed archives* available on request

Major Collections:

Public records including Grand Jury: assizes, accounts, correspondence and maps (1801–98); Poor Law Unions: minutes of the meetings of Boards of Guardians of Ballyshannon, Donegal, Dunfanaghy, Glenties, Inishowen, Letterkenny, Milford and Stranorlar Unions, indoor and outdoor relief registers, admission and discharge registers, attendance registers, medical registers including dispensary records, 1841–1923; Rural District Councils: minutes of the meetings of the Rural District Councils of Ballyshannon, Donegal, Dunfanaghy, Glenties, Inishowen, Letterkenny, Milford, Londonderry No. 2, Strabane No. 2 and Stranorlar, 1899–1925; Donegal Board of Health and Public Assistance: minutes and medical registers, 1924–42 (restricted access); Donegal County Infirmary, 19th century; Donegal County Council and Bundoran, Buncrana and Letterkenny Urban District Councils: minutes of meetings of Councils and committees; Manager's Orders; Finance, Housing, Planning, Motor Tax, Roads, Legal, Environmental, Libraries, Civil Defence, Rates and election records, 1899–1972; Ballyshannon Town Commissioners: minutes of meetings, 1896–1962, Ballyshannon Harbour Board: minutes of meetings, 1887–1962; County Donegal Committee of Agriculture: correspondence, 1901–30; Ordnance Survey: second edition maps of Donegal, 1840–81; Valuation records: including Griffith's topographical surveys and General Valuation registers, 1833–1969; Primary schools: roll books, registers, c.1880–1960s; Local Government Board: letters, 1899.

Private acquisitions: Cathal Ó Searcaigh, c.1960–90; Patrick MacGill: small collection, 1917–35; Father Patrick Gallagher: including correspondence of Donegal Historical Society, c.1940–80; Murray Stewart: family estate papers, 1749–1880; Captain Ernest Cochrane and Edward H. Harvey: mainly maps, 1865–1900; Watters Estate Agents, Milford, 1894–1967; Gweedore and Lough Swilly Hotels: visitors' books, 1842–1903; Ballybofey & Stranorlar and Templecrone Co-operative and Agricultural Societies, 1917–45; District Nursing Associations: Newtowncunningham, Burt & Killea, and Fanad, 1931–74; Andrews Linen Mills: accounts, 1895–1951; oral history: interviews taken by Anne McMenamin with elderly Donegal people; Irish Medical Association, Donegal branch, 1903–77; Lifford endowed schools, 1870–1992.

45   Donegal County Museum

Address	High Road
	Letterkenny
	County Donegal
Telephone	(074) 24613
Fax	(074) 26522
E-mail	museum@donegalcoco.ie
Enquiries to	The Curator

*Opening hours
and facilities*   Written application required for permission to consult
                       archives; photocopying

Major collections
Archives of the Archaeological Survey of Donegal.

46   Down & Connor Diocesan Archives

Address   73a Somerton Road
                       Belfast BT15 4DJ

Telephone   (02890) 776185

Enquiries to   The Diocesan Archivist

Opening hours   By appointment;
and facilities   photocopying

Major collections
Correspondence of Bishop McMullan and the Revd William McMullan,
    1803–26.
Bishop Cornelius Denvir correspondence, 1835–65.
Archbishop William Crolly of Armagh correspondence, 1835–49.
Bishop Daniel Mageean correspondence, 1929–62.
Bishop William Philbin correspondence, 1962–82.

47   Down County Museum

Address   The Mall
                       Downpatrick
                       County Down BT30 6AH

Telephone   (02844) 615218

Fax   (02844) 615590

Enquiries to   The Keeper of Collections

Opening hours   10.00–5.00, Tues–Fri; 2.00–5.00, Sat;
and facilities   10.00–5.00, Mon (June–Aug);
                       2.00–5.00, Sun (June–Aug) photocopying; photography

Major collections
The collections in the museum relate to County Down from the prehistoric

period to the present and include documents associated with the collections: certificates, minute books, maps and plans.
Photographic archive.

48   Drogheda Borough Council

Address	Council Offices
	Fair Street
	Drogheda
	County Louth
Telephone	(041) 987 6100
Fax	(041) 983 9306
E-mail	tclerk@droghedaboro.ie
Website	www.droghedaboro.ie
Enquiries to	The Town Clerk
Opening hours and facilities	9.00–1.00, 2.00–5.00, Mon–Fri, by appointment; photocopying

Major collections
Charters: James II, 1687; William III, 1697; George I, *c.*1725; William IV, 1833.
Council Book (minutes), October 1649–.
Freedom Books, 1690–.
Maps: Newcomen's map of Drogheda, 1657; Ravell's map of Drogheda, 1749; Skinner and Taylor's map of Drogheda, 1778; Greene's map of Drogheda, 1878.

49   Drogheda Port Company

Address	Maritime House
	The Mall
	Drogheda
Telephone	(041) 983 8378/983 6026
Fax	(041) 983 2844
E-mail	maritimehouse@droghedaport.ie
Enquiries to	The Secretary & Chief Executive

| *Opening hours* | 9.00–5.00, Mon–Thur; 9.00–4.45, Fri; |
| *and facilities* | photocopying; photography |

Major collections
Minute books, 1790–.

50   Dromore Diocesan Archives

Address	Bishop's House
	Newry
	County Down
Telephone	(028) 3026 2444
Fax	(028) 3026 0496
Enquiries to	The Bishop of Dromore
Opening hours	By appointment;
and facilities	photocopying;

Major collections
Correspondence and papers of bishops, 1770–.
Records of baptisms, marriages and deaths for each parish, 1926–.
Other diocesan and parish papers.

51   Dublin City Archives

Address	Dublin City Library and Archive
	138–144 Pearse Street
	Dublin 2
Telephone	(01) 674 4800
Fax	(01) 674 4881
E-mail	cityarchives@dublincity.ie
Website	www.dublincity.ie
Enquiries to	The City Archivist
Opening hours	10.00–8.00, Mon–Thur; 10.00–5.00, Fri–Sat;
and facilities	photocopying; photography

Guides	Sir John T. and Lady Gilbert (eds), *Calendar of ancient records of Dublin* (19 vols, Dublin 1889–1944); Mary Clark, *The book of maps of the Dublin city surveyors* (1983); Niall McCullough, *A vision of the city: Dublin and the Wide Streets Commissioners (*1991*);* Philomena Connolly and Geoffrey Martin, *The Dublin guild merchant roll* (1992); Mary Clark and Raymond Refaussé, *Directory of historic Dublin guilds* (1993); Mary Clark and Gráinne Doran, *Serving the city: the Dublin city managers and town clerks* (1996); Colm Lennon and James Murray, *The Dublin city franchise roll* (1998); Jane Ohlmeyer and Eamonn O Ciardha, *The Irish statute staple books* (1998)

Major collections

Principal civic collections: Royal charters of the city of Dublin, 1171–1727; medieval cartularies, including Liber Albus and Chain Book of Dublin; Dublin City Assembly Rolls, 1447–1841; Board of Dublin Aldermen, 1567–1841; journals of sheriffs and commons, 1746–1841; Tholsell Court of Dublin, 16th–18th centuries; Dublin City treasurer's accounts, 1540–1841; Freedom records, 1468–1918; City surveyor's maps, 1695–1928; minutes and reports of Dublin City Council, 1841–; photographic collection, including Liffey Bridges and North Strand bombing; records of Dublin Corporation committees and departments, 1840–1970; electoral registers, 1937–.

Other collections: records of some trade and religious guilds to 1841; Wide Streets Commission, 1757–1849; Paving Board, 1774–1840; charitable committees, including Mansion House Relief Fund, 1880; Rathmines and Rathgar Township, 1847–1930; Pembroke Township, 1863–1930; Civics Institute of Ireland, 1918–60.

52   Dublin City Public Libraries
Dublin and Irish Collections

Address	Dublin City Library and Archive 138–144 Pearse Street Dublin 2
Telephone	(01) 674 4800
Fax	(01) 674 4881
E-mail	dublinstudies@dublincity.ie

Website	www.dublincity.ie
Enquiries to	Divisional Librarian, Special Collections
Opening hours and facilities	10.00–8.00, Mon–Thur; 10.00–5.00, Fri–Sat; photocopying; photography
Guides	Douglas Hyde & D.J. O'Donoghue (comps), *Catalogue of the books & manuscripts comprising the library of the late Sir John T. Gilbert* (1918)

Major collections

286 manuscripts and transcripts of manuscripts, collected by, or transcribed for, Sir John T. Gilbert in connection with his work on the history of the City of Dublin and on Irish history. The Robinson MSS, *c.*1740–60, the notebooks and other documents of an Irish judge, are of interest in that they deal with notable law cases in which Mr Justice Robinson was involved. The collection of letters addressed to Richard Caulfield, 1848–60, cover topics connected with Irish topography and genealogy. James Goddard's 'Complete abstract of Deeds belonging to the Guild of St Anne' includes material on Dublin parishes and trade guilds. Transcripts include the Assembly Rolls of Dublin, 1660–1803, charters and documents of the Guild of the Holy Trinity or Merchant Guild of Dublin, 1438–1824, and other guilds of the city; and a transcript of the Book of Charters belonging to the City of Dublin. Some transcripts are of documents which have since been destroyed or disappeared (e.g. copies of letters on state affairs in Ireland, from the Phillipps Collection – the originals were destroyed in a fire in 1711).

Dublin and Irish Collections.

Manuscript leases relating to Dublin properties.

53   Dublin Diocesan Archives

Address	Archbishop's House Drumcondra Dublin 9
Telephone	(01) 837 9253
Fax	(01) 836 8393
E-mail	dco@iol.ie
Enquiries to	The Archivist

Opening hours and facilities	9.30–1.00, 2.00–5.30, Mon–Fri; by appointment; photocopying; photography
Guides	Calendars of the papers of Archbishop Murray (1823–52) have been published in *Archivium Hibernicum* 36–42 (including an index). For a general overview see David C. Sheehy, 'Dublin Diocesan Archives – an introduction', *Archivium Hibernicum* 42 (1987)

Major collections

Papers of the Roman Catholic archbishops of Dublin, *c.*1750–.

Papers of bishops (auxiliary), priests and lay persons, 1820–.

Diocesan (chapter) records, 1729–.

Minutes of meetings of bishops, 1829–49; 1882.

Combined surviving records of the Catholic Board, the Catholic Association and the Repeal Association, 1806–47.

Papers of Dr Bartholomew Woodlock, rector of the Catholic University, 1854–79.

Records of Holy Cross College, Clonliffe, 1867–1946.

54   Dublin Port Company

Address	Port Centre Alexandra Road Dublin 1
Telephone	(01) 855 0888
Fax	(01) 855 1241
E-mail	dubport@dublin–port.ie
Website	www.dublinport.ie
Enquiries to	The Archivist
Opening hours and facilities	10.00–5.00, Wed; by appointment; photocopying

Major collections

Letters and documents, early 1860s–. Maps, early 1800s–. General ledgers, 1801–. Records of engineers, early 1900s–. Archives of the Customs House Docks, 1830s–, and of the Engineer's Department, 1905–. Arrivals and sailings, early 1930s–. Photographs of activity in the port and news-cuttings concerning the port.

55   Dublin Writers Museum

Address	18 Parnell Square North Dublin 1
Telephone	(01) 872 2077
Fax	(01) 872 2231
E-mail	writers@dublintourism.ie
Website	www.visitdublin.com
Enquiries to	The Curator
Opening hours and facilities	10.00–5.00, Mon–Sat; 11.00–5.00, Sun & public holidays; access to archives by appointment only

Major collections
Papers relating to Cornelius Ryan, Geoffrey Phibbs, Norah McGuinness, Bram Stoker, George Russell (Æ) and Lennox Robinson.

56   Dún Laoghaire–Rathdown County Council

Address	County Hall Marine Road Dún Laoghaire County Dublin
Telephone	(01) 205 4743/ 205 4700
Fax	(01) 280 6969
E-mail	corp@dlrcoco.ie
Website address	www.dlrcoco.ie
Enquiries to	The Senior Staff Officer, Corporate Services
Opening hours and facilities	Appointment necessary; photocopying

Major collections
Archives of Dún Laoghaire Corporation, 1930–73, including archives of the townships and urban district councils of Blackrock, Dalkey, Killiney-

Ballybrack and Dún Laoghaire, mid-19th century–1930; records of the Dean's Grange Joint Burial Board.

Archives of that area of the former Dublin County Council now within the jurisdiction of Dún Laoghaire–Rathdown County Council are in the custody of Fingal County Archives (q.v.).

57   Dunsink Observatory

Address	Castleknock Dublin 15
Telephone	(01) 838 7911/838 7959
Fax	(01) 838 7090
E-mail	astro@dunsink.dias.ie
Enquiries to	The Director
Opening hours and facilities	By appointment; photocopying; photography

Major collections

Miscellaneous astronomy documents, 1790–1850. Correspondence and minutes, 1947–87, held at Dublin Institute for Advanced Studies, 10 Burlington Road, Dublin 4.

58   Elphin Diocesan Archives

Address	Diocesan Office St Mary's Sligo
Telephone	(071) 62670
Fax	(071) 62414
E-mail	elphindo@eircom.ie
Website	www.elphindiocese.ie
Enquiries to	The Diocesan Secretary
Opening hours and facilities	By appointment; photocopying

Major collections
Correspondence of Bishops Laurence Gillooly, John Clancy, Bernard Coyne, Edward Doorly and Vincent Hanly, 1858–1970. Some historical data on parishes in Elphin diocese.

59   Enniskillen Library

Address	Hall's Lane
	Enniskillen
	County Fermanagh BT74 7DR
	Northern Ireland
Telephone	(02866) 322886
Fax	(02866) 324685
E-mail	enniskillen_library@welbni.org
Website	www.welbni.org/libraries/homepage.htm
Enquiries to	The Assistant Librarian for Local Studies
Opening hours and facilities	9.15–5.15, Mon, Wed, Fri; 9.15–7.30, Tue, Thur; 9.15–1.00, Sat; photocopying, microfilm reader-printer

Major collections
Nawn Collection of local studies material includes photographs and maps as well as a substantial collection of books, prints, periodicals and paintings; and special collections relating to railway and military history.
Copies of census and valuation records of local interest.
Records of public elementary schools in County Fermanagh, mainly roll books for schools in the Clones area.

60   Erasmus Smith Trust Archives

Address	Danum
	Zion Road
	Rathgar
	Dublin 6
Telephone	(01) 492 2611
Fax	(01) 492 4427

E-mail	archives@highschooldublin.com
Website	www.highschooldublin.com/erasmus.htm
Enquiries to	The Archivist
Opening hours and facilities	Enquiries by post, telephone, fax or e-mail

Major collections

Administrative records of 'The Governors of the Schools founded by Erasmus Smith Esq.' including: legal papers, 1671–1959; accounts, 1673–*c.*1970; minutes of the Board of Governors, 1674–*c.*1970; material relating to scholarships, exhibitions and appointments in Trinity College, Dublin, 1712–1951; minutes of the Standing Committee, 1803–1961; letter books, 1810–1951 and correspondence, 1850–*c.*1970.

Records of the Trust's estates including: rentals, 1658–*c.*1970; maps, 1711–1971; valuations, *c.*1815–1947; correspondence, 1859–*c.*1970; land agents' letter books, 1862–1911; Southern Estate leases and property deeds, 1672–1966; Western Estate leases and property deeds, 1667–*c.*1970; Irish Land Commission, 1879–1937.

Records of the Trust's grammar schools: Drogheda Grammar School, 1680–1956; Galway Grammar School, 1715–1962; Tipperary Grammar School (The Abbey School), 1760–1939; Ennis Grammar School, 1832–1930; and The High School, Dublin, 1870–.

Records of the English Schools [primary schools funded by the Trust and located in all counties except Leitrim] including architectural plans (for 64 buildings), leases and maps, 1803–1920; masters' and inspectors' reports, 1851–1936; and correspondence, 1824–1947.

Material relating to secondary schools aided by the Trust including: Christ's Hospital, London, 1651–*c.*1912; King's Hospital, Dublin, 1807–1941; and Great Brunswick Street Commercial School, Dublin, 1871–1899.

61   ESB Archives

Address	Parnell Avenue Harold's Cross Dublin 6
Telephone	(01) 604 2132
Fax	(01) 604 2133
Enquiries to	The Archives Manager/Team Leader Archives

Opening hours   9.30–12.30, 2.00–4.00, Mon–Fri; by appointment
and facilities

Major collections
Archives relating to the history and development of electricity supply in
Ireland with particular reference to the Rural Electrification Scheme and
to individual power stations. Film, photographs and memorabilia. Oral
history collection of interviews with retired members of staff.

62   Fermanagh County Museum

Address	Castle Barracks Enniskillen County Fermanagh
Telephone	(02866) 325000
Fax	(02866) 327342
E-mail	castle@fermanagh.gov.uk
Website	enniskillencastle.co.uk
Enquiries to	The Museum Officer
Opening hours and facilities	2.00–5.00, Mon, 10.00–5.00, Tue–Fri; photocopying; photography

Major collections
Local Government: County Fermanagh landholding and sales posters;
County Assize proclamations.
Genealogy: correspondence of Lady Dorothy Lowry-Corry, 1931–5; family
records of Canon W.H. Dundas (d. 1941). 17th-century documents:
appointment of Hamilton as governor of Enniskillen, 1689; letter from
Schomberg to Wynne, 1689; commission of Major J. Folliott as major in
the dragoons, 1689.
Photographic collection comprising almost 10,000 negatives, glass plates,
copy and original prints, *c.*1850–, depicting ancient monuments, archaeology, folklife, work and recreation, transport, military and police, and
the landscape and wildlife of the locality.
Ephemera dealing with entertainment, sport, politics, religion and organizations in County Fermanagh.
Porter estate papers, 19th–20th century. Archdale estate rentals and accounts,
1904–23.

63 Fingal County Archives

Address	11 Parnell Square
	Dublin 1
Telephone	(01) 872 7968
Fax	(01) 878 6919
E-mail	fincolib@iol.ie
Website	www.iol.ie/~fincolib/
Enquiries to	The Archivist
Opening hours	10.00–1.00, 2.00–4.30, Mon–Fri; appointment necessary; photocopying
Guides	Introductory leaflets

Major collections

Records of Dublin County Council, 1898–1993; records of rural and urban district councils including Dublin North, 1901–30, Dublin South, 1899–1930, and Howth, 1918–40. Grand Jury records, 1818–98.

Records of the Dublin Board of Public Health, 1930–42, and Dublin County Committee of Agriculture and Technical Instruction, 1908–72.

Records of Balbriggan Town Commissioners, 1860–1995.

Records of Townpike Roads including Dublin to Dunleer, 1775–1856; Dublin to Mullingar, 1792–1856; Dublin to Malahide, 1826–55; Dublin to Carlow, 1829–59; Dublin to Navan, 1800–48; Dublin to Drogheda, 1849–55; and Dublin to Knocksedan, 1798–1856.

Private collections including records of Cloghran Stud Farm, 1954–89; and records of the Cuffe family of Swords, 1797–1933.

64 Franciscan Library, Killiney

Address	Dún Mhuire
	Seafield Road
	Killiney
	County Dublin
Telephone	(01) 282 6760/ 282 6091
Fax	(01) 282 6993

Enquiries to	The Librarian
Opening hours and facilities	By appointment; photocopying
Guides	G.D. Burtchaell and J.M. Rigg, *Report on Franciscan manuscripts preserved at the Convent, Merchants' Quay, Dublin* (1906); M. Dillon, C. Mooney OFM, P. de Brún, *Catalogue of Irish manuscripts in the Franciscan Library, Killiney* (Dublin Institute for Advanced Studies, 1969). C. Mooney OFM, 'Franciscan Library, Killiney: a short guide', *Archivium Hibernicum* 18 (1955), 150–6; C. Schmitt OFM, 'Manuscrits de la "Franciscan Library" de Killiney', *Archivum Franciscanum Historicum* 57 (1964), 165–90; Ignatius Fennessy OFM, 'The B manuscripts in the Franciscan Library, Killiney' in B. Millett and A. Lynch (eds.) *Dún Mhuire, Killiney, 1945–95* (1995), 150–215

Major collections

Irish Franciscan manuscripts, 17th–20th century, including papers relating to Irish Franciscan houses in Ireland and in Europe, and collections such as the Wadding Papers; Irish historical manuscripts 17th–20th century, such as the Hayes Papers on the Veto Question; Franciscan historical and theological papers, 15th–17th century.

The custody of the collection of Gaelic manuscripts designated 'A' MSS formerly housed in the FLK, including the 'Psalter of St Caimin', Liber Hymnorum, Martyrology of Tallaght (Book of Leinster) and Annals of the Four Masters, has been transferred to University College Dublin Archives Department (*q.v.*) under the terms of a partnership agreement between the OFM and UCD.

65   The Gaelic Athletic Association Museum

Address	Croke Park Dublin 3
Telephone	(01) 855 8176
Fax	(01) 855 8104
E-mail	museum@crokepark.ie

Enquiries to	The Museum Administrator
Opening hours and facilities	9.30–5.00, Mon–Sat, 12.00–5.00, Sun stadium tours run on a daily basis

Major collections

A large collection of documents, memorabilia and photographs from the foundation of the Association in 1884 to the present, including minutes of meetings, programmes and printed matter.

Much of the collection is on display to the general public. An archive, and a photographic and reference library will be open to the public in the near future.

66   Galway County Council Archives & Galway County Libraries

Address	Galway County Libraries Headquarters Island House Cathedral Square Galway
Telephone	(091) 562471
Fax	(091) 565039
E-mail	pmcwalter@galwaycoco.ie
Enquiries to	The Archivist
Opening hours and facilities	Appointment necessary; photocopying

Major Collections

Galway County Council records including minutes, 1899–; Manager's Orders, 1942–; valuation lists, *c.*1896–1988; Galway Board of Health & Public Assistance, 1922–44; Galway County Libraries collection, 1924–98; bog expenditure and turf haulage ledgers, 1941–51; minutes of various committees such as County Education Committee, 1911–64, Loughrea Waterworks Committee, 1903–33, National Monuments Advisory Committee, 1947–89; Registers of Electors, 1964–; Burial Ground Registers, 1922–2002; Registers of Scholarship Awards, 1917–72.

Galway Infirmary Governors minutes, 1839–92; Galway Hospital minutes, registers and accounts, 1892–1932; Galway Hospital Nursing Committee minutes, 1904–22.

Ballinasloe Town Commissioners records, 1840–1917, and Ballinasloe Urban District Council records, 1880–1990.

Poor Law Union collections: Ballinasloe, 1842–1921, Clifden, 1849–1921, Galway, 1839–1937, Glenamaddy, 1894–1914, Gort, 1844–1920, Loughrea, 1839–1922, Mountbellew, 1850–1921, Portumna, 1881–84, and Tuam, 1839–1926.

Rural District Council collections: Ballinasloe No. 1, 1899–1925, Ballinasloe No. 2, 1917–19, Clifden, 1899–1925, Galway, 1904–25, Gort, 1899–1925, Loughrea, 1901–25, Mountbellew, 1899–1923, Portumna, 1900–25, and Tuam, 1907–25.

Small and private collections including Blakes of Brooklodge, Ballygluinn, Tuam, 1666–1934; ffrench of Rahasane, Loughrea, 1765–1897; Cecil R. Henry, Toghermore, Tuam, 1882–94; Mark Lynch, Galway town, 1785–1804; McDonnell merchants, Dunmore, County Galway 1897–1904; O'Kelly of Castle Kelly, Ballygar, 1606–1880; Charles O'Rorke, baronies of Ballymoe & Dunmore, 1904–31; Shawe-Taylor of Castle Taylor, Ardrahan, 1890–1909; St George Mansergh, Headford, 1775–1853; Galway Mechanics Institute, 1862–1977; Garavan's Public House, Shop Street, Galway, 1945–57; Grealy's Medical Hall, Dispensing Chemists, William Street, Galway, 1888–1962; Irish Sugar Company, Tuam, 1934–87; P.M. Kavanagh, Dispensing Chemist and Fahy Chemist, High Street, Galway, 1919–88; William Lawrence, Lisreaghan or Belview, Lawrencetown, 1882, family album; Galway Courthouse, drawings and plans, 1870.

67   Galway Diocesan Archives

Address	The Cathedral Galway
Telephone	(091) 563566
Fax	(091) 568333
Enquiries to	The Archivist
Opening hours and facilities	By appointment

Major collections

Matters dealing with Galway diocese.

Documents and correspondence in relation to the diocese of Galway, Kilmacduagh and Kilfenora.

68   Galway Harbour Company

Address	New Docks Galway
Telephone	(091) 562329/561874
Fax	(091) 563738
E-mail	info@galwayharbour.com
Enquiries to	The CEO
Opening hours	9.30–5.30, Mon–Fri; photocopying. National University of Ireland, Galway (q.v.) holds microfilm copies of Galway Harbour Commissioners records which may be consulted with written permission from Galway Harbour Company.

Major collections

Minute books, 1833–1997; arrivals and departures book, 1872–1901; tonnage and imports dues book 1884–1914; export dues book, 1882–1914; general maintenance and wages ledger, 1830–67; printed abstracts of accounts, 1854–1934.

69   Gamble Library

Address	Union Theological College of the Presbyterian Church in Ireland 108 Botanic Avenue Belfast BT7 1JT
Telephone	(02890) 205093
Fax	(02890) 316839
E-mail	librarian@union.ac.uk
Enquiries to	The Librarian
Opening hours and facilities	9.00–5.00, Mon–Thur; 9.00–4.30, Fri; appointment necessary; photocopying

Major collections

Presbytery and synod minutes of the Presbyterian Church in Ireland, 17th–19th century.

70   Garda Museum/Archives
Garda Síochána na hÉireann

Address	Record Tower Dublin Castle Dublin 2
Telephone	(01) 666 9998
E-mail	gatower@iol.ie
Website address	www.policehistory.com
Enquiries to	The Curator
Opening hours and facilities	9.30–4.30, Mon–Sun; appointment advisable for Sat & Sun;

Major collections

The Museum displays historical material relating to the Royal Irish Constabulary, Dublin Metropolitan Police and An Garda Síochána, including uniforms, medals, photographs, certificates of merit and a small collection of private family letters.

The reading room contains RIC directories, guides and codes of instruction [service records are available on microfilm in the National Archives (q.v)]; DMP membership register, 1836–1925, and some personal records of membership, photographs, guides and codes of instruction and material relating to the early history of the Garda Síochána, as well as photographs and publications.

71   Genealogical Office

Address	2 Kildare Street Dublin 2
Telephone	(01) 603 0311
Fax	(01) 662 1062
E-mail	herald@nli.ie
Website address	www.nli.ie
Enquiries to	The Chief Herald/Deputy Chief Herald

Opening hours and facilities	Access to the collections may be had through the Manuscripts Reading Room of the National Library (q.v.), 10.00–8.30, Mon–Wed; 10.00–4.30, Thur–Fri; 10.00–12.30, Sat
Guides	List of Genealogical Office manuscripts 1–822 available in the Manuscript Reading Room; some material listed in R.J. Hayes (ed.), *Manuscript sources for the history of Irish civilisation* (1965); P.B. Eustace, 'Index of the will abstracts in the Genealogical Office', *Analecta Hibernica* 17 (1949); J. Barry, 'Guide to records of the Genealogical Office, Dublin', *Analecta Hibernica* 26 (1970).

Major collections

Registers of arms, 16th century–.

Registrations of pedigrees, 16th century–.

Heraldic visitations, mainly of Counties Dublin and Wexford, 16th–17th century.

Sixteen volumes of funeral entries, 17th century.

Lords' Entry volumes (records relating to the introduction of peers to the Irish House of Lords), 18th century.

Records of the Order of St Patrick (founded 1783).

Records of Sir William Beetham especially his abstracts from Irish prerogative wills (30 volumes) and pedigrees (23 volumes).

Administrative records of the office of Ulster King of Arms.

Family genealogies, various. Loose pedigrees.

72   General Register Office/ Oifig An Ard–Chláraitheora

Address	Joyce House 8/11 Lombard Street East Dublin 2
Telephone	(01) 635 0000/ 635 4430/ 635 4417
Fax	(01) 635 4440/ 635 4527
E-mail	Website responder form
Website	www.groireland.ie
Enquiries to	Ard–Chláraitheoir Cúnta

Opening hours and facilities	9.30–12.30, 2.15–4.30, Mon–Fri; photocopying and certified copies of entries

Major collections

Registers of births registered in all Ireland, 1 Jan 1864–31 Dec 1921, and in Ireland (exclusive of the six north-eastern counties) from that date. Registers of deaths registered in all Ireland, 1 Jan 1864–31 Dec 1921, and in Ireland (exclusive of the six north–eastern counties) from that date. Registers of marriages in all Ireland, 1 Apr 1845–31 Dec 1863, except those celebrated by the Roman Catholic clergy.

Registers of all marriages registered in the whole of Ireland, 1 Jan 1864–1 Dec 1921, and in Ireland (exclusive of the six north-eastern counties) from that date.

Note: Only the indexes to the above records are open to public inspection, on payment of appropriate fee. Clients may purchase copies of individual entries identified in the Index.

73   General Register Office, Northern Ireland

Address	Oxford House 49/55 Chichester Street Belfast BTI 4HL
Telephone	(02890) 252021/2/3/4
Fax	(02890) 252120
E-mail	gro.nisra@dfpni.gov.uk
Website address	www.groni.gov.uk
Enquiries to	The Deputy Registrar General
Opening hours and facilities	9.30–4.00, Mon–Fri, except the first Tuesday of each month, 10.00–4.00; copying
Guides	Information leaflets including *Records and search services*

Major collections

Records of births and deaths held in the General Register Office relate mainly to those registered since 1 Jan 1864 in that part of Ireland which is now Northern Ireland.

Marriage records are available in this office from 1922 only.

For information on a marriage which occurred subsequent to civil registration and prior to 1922 application should be made to the District Registrar, addresses of whom are obtainable from the General Register Office.

There are two types of General Search available: 1. Assisted search – a general search of the records assisted by members of GRO staff for any period of years and any number of entries; 2. Index Search – computerised indexes are available for searching with limited verification of entries by staff.

74   Geological Survey of Ireland

Address	Beggars Bush Haddington Road Dublin 4
Telephone	(01) 678 2000
Fax	(01) 668 1782
E-mail	tonyglackin@gsi.ie
Website address	www.gsi.ie
Enquiries to	The Public Office
Opening hours and facilities	Public Office 9.30–4.30, Mon–Thur, 9.30–3.30, Fri; photocopying

Major collections

Geological Survey of Ireland field sheets: original six-inch to the mile (1:10, 560) geological field maps of the 26 counties, 1845–87 and early 20th-century six-inch glacial drift/land use maps of Cork, Dublin and Limerick city areas.

Geological Survey of Ireland archives: miscellaneous manuscripts from the Portlock Survey, 1820s–40s; Geological Survey of Ireland correspondence books, 1845–*c.*1900; du Noyer geological drawings, 1836–69; and printed material, including a reference set of geological maps of Ireland (largely 19th century) and pre–1900 geological books, from the Geological Survey library and the Portlock Bequest.

75   Geological Survey of Northern Ireland

Address	20 College Gardens Belfast BT9 6BS

Telephone	(02890) 666595
E-mail	gsni@bgs.ac.uk
Website	www.bgs.ac.uk/gsni
Enquiries to	The Director
Opening hours and facilities	9.00–4.30, Mon–Fri; photocopying
Guides	Regional Geology Guide to Northern Ireland

Major collections

6" geological field maps of the 19th-century Geological Survey of Ireland relating to Northern Ireland.

6" to 1 mile and 1:10,000 scale field maps of the Geological Survey of Northern Ireland, 1947–.

Library reference collection of maps, scientific papers, reports and records relating to the geology of Northern Ireland.

76   Glenstal Abbey

Address	Murroe County Limerick
Telephone	(061) 386103
Fax	(061) 386328
Enquiries to	The Archivist
Opening hours and facilities	Postal enquiry only

Major collections

Non-monastic: Carbery papers, 1658–1759; Sir Thomas Hackett papers, 1688–1720; Cloncurry papers, 1880–1909; correspondence between Mother Mary Martin and Bede Lebbe, 1930s; Fr John Sweetman papers, 1911–23; diaries of Richard Hobart, 1784–1802, Sir Thomas Kane, 1837, and J. Grene Barry, 1869–76; Gaelic League Ard-Craomh minute book, 1907–15.

Monastic: foundation correspondence; legal and administrative documents; financial, farm and school records; seniorate minute books, 1927–80; material relating to congresses, 1952–; material relating to the foundation in Nigeria, 1974–; private papers of deceased monks.

77   Company of Goldsmiths

Address	Goldsmiths Hall Assay Office Dublin Castle Dublin 2
Telephone	(01) 475 1286/478 0323;
Fax	(01) 478 3838
E-mail	hallmark@assay.ie
Enquiries to	The Assay Master
Opening hours and facilities	8.30–12.00, 1.00–3.45, Mon–Fri; by appointment
Guides	M. Clark & R. Refaussé (eds), *Directory of historic Dublin guilds* (1993)

Major collections
Archives of the Guild of All Saints (Goldsmiths) including: charter, 1637; minutes and work ledgers, 1637–; records of freemen, apprentices, brethren and members, 17th–19th century; accounts, 17th–20th century; letter books and certificates, 19th century.
The collection is available on microfilm in the National Library of Ireland.

78   Good Shepherd Sisters

Address	Pennywell Road Limerick
Telephone	(061) 415178
Fax	(061) 415147
Enquiries to	The Archivist
Opening hours and facilities	By appointment or postal enquiry; photocopying

Major collections
Papers relating to the general government of the congregation including the constitution and proceedings of general chapters and commissions; papers of successive superiors general and their councils;

Papers relating to the constitution and government of the province, 1862–, including proceedings of provincial chapters and inter–provincial meetings, 1869–; papers of provincial superiors and councils, 1869–; material relating to provincial policy and commissions; correspondence, accounts, statistics, annals and publications, 1870–.

Records of Limerick Convent, 1848–, including St Mary's Home, 1837–1976; St Joseph's Reformatory School, 1859–1972; St George's Industrial School, 1869–1970; group homes for children in care, hostels, shelters, and community service.

Records of convents, now closed, in New Ross, 1860–1967; Newry, 1944–84; Dunboyne, 1955–91

Photographs, press cuttings and reference material.

79   Guinness Archive, Diageo Ireland

Address	Guinness Storehouse St James's Gate Dublin 8
Telephone	(01) 471 4557
E-mail	guinness.archives@diageo.com
Enquiries to	The Archivist
Opening hours and facilities	9.30–5.00 Mon–Thur, 9.30–4.30 Fri; access to primary material by appointment only; photocopying

Major collections

Guinness annual reports, 1886–; Board minutes, 1886–1960s; Board memoranda, endorsements and orders, 1886–1960s; correspondence with Lord Iveagh, 1910–36; departmental annual and weekly reports, 1898–1940s. Departmental files reflecting overall working of the St James's Gate Brewery, early 1800s–, including: brewers' calculation books, 19th and 20th century; engineering project files, *c.*1900–60s; individual employee records, 1880s–1950s, trade records and ledgers. Photographs of brewery buildings, brewing process, personnel, 1880s–. Brewery maps, 1820–. Advertising collection consisting of film, videos, posters, press ads, bottles, cans, dripmats, labels for all Guinness brands.

Printed matter: Guinness brewery guidebooks, 1880 to present; overseas travellers reports, 1899–1914; Guinness laboratory reports, 1898–1910; Guinness Chemists Laboratory reports, 1904–48; Guinness Hop

Farm annual reports, 1906–26; Company magazines, 1958–present. Comprehensive research library containing publications on the history of Guinness and the Guinness family, history of brewing, *Journal of the Institute of Brewing,* 1895–1979, *Guinness book of records,* 1955–2001

Non-Company-related collections: Charter of the Coopers' Guild granted by Charles II, 1666. Minute books and papers of the Coopers' Guild of Dublin, 1765–1976. Minute books of Robert Perry and Sons Ltd, 1928–53. Minutes and accounts of the British Association for the Advancement of Science, Dublin, 1956–8.

The High School, Dublin *see* Erasmus Smith Trust Archives

80   Holy Faith Sisters (Sisters of the Holy Faith)

Address	Holy Faith Convent Glasnevin Dublin 11
Telephone	(01) 837 3427
E-mail	aylward@eircom.net
	gemmagilroy@eircom.net
Enquiries to	The Archivist
Opening hours and facilities	By appointment; photocopying

Major collections
Correspondence of founders, Margaret Aylward and Fr John Gowan CM, 1840s–. Life and lectures of Fr Gowan. Life and spiritual notes of John Joseph Steiner, a German convert and collector for St Brigid's Orphanage. Files relating to each convent of the Congregation including those in the Mission Fields. Aylward family papers. Personal effects of founders.

81   Holy Ghost Congregation (Irish Province)

Address	Temple Park Richmond Avenue South Dublin 6
Telephone	(01) 497 5127/497 7230/412 5230
Fax	(01) 497 5399
E-mail	archivespiritan@eircom.net
Enquiries to	The Archivist
Opening hours and facilities	By appointment; photocopying

Major collections
Material relating to the origins of the Congregation in Ireland; to its work at home including Blackrock College, Rockwell College, St Mary's College, Rathmines, St Michael's College, Ailesbury Road, Templeogue College, and Kimmage Manor Seminary and Institute; and on the foreign missions including Nigeria, Sierra Leone, The Gambia, Kenya, Malawi, South Africa, Australia, Angola, Brazil, Ethiopia, Mauritius, Pakistan, Canada, Tanzania, Uganda, Zambia, Papua New Guinea, USA, Botswana, Ghana and Liberia.

82   Hugh Lane Municipal Gallery of Modern Art

Address	Charlemont House Parnell Square Dublin 1
Telephone	(01) 874 1903
Fax	(01) 872 2182
E-mail	info@hughlane.ie
Website address	www.hughlane.ie
Enquiries to	The Director
Opening hours	Access to archives is by postal enquiry only

Major collections
Papers of Ellen Duncan, first Curator of the Gallery, 1914–22.
Archives of the Gallery, 1939–90.
Photographic collection, *c.*1907–90.
Papers of Harry Clarke (1889–1931), stained glass artist.

83 Incorporated Law Society of Ireland

Address	Blackhall Place Dublin 7
Telephone	(01) 672 4800
Fax	(01) 672 4801
Website address	www.lawsociety.ie
Enquiries to	The Librarian
Opening hours and facilities	8.30–5.30, Mon–Fri; by appointment; photocopying

Major collections
Minute books of meetings of Council, 1922–.

84 Infant Jesus Sisters – Nicolas Barré

Address	56 St Lawrence Road Clontarf Dublin 3
Telephone	(01) 833 9577
Fax	(01) 853 0857
Enquiries to	The Archivist
Opening hours and facilities	Postal enquiry only; main congregational archives located in Paris; photocopying

Major collections
Material relating to the history of the Infant Jesus Sisters in Ireland, 1909–,
    and England, 1892–; to the educational Apostolate of the Irish Sisters in

Malaysia, Singapore, Japan, Australia, USA, Nigeria, the Cameroons and Peru; to the Founder, Venerable Nicholas Barré, and to the general history of the Institute, 1662–. Includes correspondence, photographs, reports of meetings and councils, and account books from the farm, brush factories, sawmills and knitting factories set up in Ireland in the early 20th century to combat emigration.

85 Institution of Engineers of Ireland

Address	22 Clyde Road Ballsbridge Dublin 4
Telephone	(01) 668 4341
Fax	(01) 668 5508
E-mail	library@iei.ie
Website	www.iei.ie
Enquiries to	The Librarian
Opening hours and facilities	9.00–5.00, Mon–Fri; photocopying
Guides	N. Hughes, *Index to the Transactions of the Institution of Engineers of Ireland, 1845–1991* (Dublin, 1992)

Major collections
Transactions of the Institution of Engineers of Ireland, 1845–1991.
Correspondence and reports of the eminent railway engineer John MacNeill, 1826–44.

86 The Irish Agricultural Museum

Address	Johnstown Castle Old Farmyard Wexford County Wexford
Telephone	(053) 42888
Fax	(053) 42213

E-mail AOSULLIVAN@johnstown.teagasc.ie

Enquiries to The Curator

Opening hours By appointment;
and facilities photocopying

Major collections

Small amount of mill account books and estate records, mostly from County
Wexford, *c.*1850–1900. Malting industry records for Wexford and
Castlebridge.

Machinery manufacturers' catalogues from Ireland, Great Britain and North
America, 1900–50.

87 Irish Architectural Archive

Address 73 Merrion Square
Dublin 2
from June 2004
45 Merrion Square
Dublin 2

Telephone (01) 676 3430

Fax (01) 676 6309

E-mail info@iarc.ie

Website address www.iarc.ie

Enquiries to The Archive Administrator or Archive Director

Opening hours 10.00–1.00, 2.30–5.00, Tue–Fri;
and facilities photocopying; photography

Major collections

The Irish Architectural Archive collects, preserves and makes available
records of every type relating to the architecture of Ireland. The holdings
comprise in excess of 150,000 architectural drawings, 320,000 photographs, 15,000 items of printed matter and several dozen architectural
models, 1690s–. The collections include information on every notable
Irish architect, on every important Irish building period or style, and on
most significant buildings in Ireland.

Major collections include: Ashlin & Coleman; Boyd Barrett Murphy
O'Connor; Burgage; Rudolph Maximilian Butler; Charleville Forest;

Maurice Craig; Cullen & Company; C.P. Curran; Dublin Artisans Dwellings Company; Emo Court; Desmond Featherstone; Desmond FitzGerald; Charles Geoghan; Guinness Drawings; Alan Hope; Brendan Jeffers; Alfred Jones Biographical Index; W.A. Johnston, Simon J. Kelly & Partners; Lundy; McCurdy & Mitchell; Raymond McGrath; Niall Montgomery & Partners; Munden & Purcell; Donal O'Neill Flanagan; Patterson Kempster Shortall; Anthony Reddy & Associates; Frederick Rogerson; RIAI Murray Collection; Royal (Collins) Barracks; Royal Institute of the Architects of Ireland Archives; Robinson Keefe & Devane; Scott Tallon Walker; Michael Scott; Sibthorpe; Stephenson Gibney; Townley Hall; Tyndall Hogan Hurley; Workhouse Collection.

Photographic collections include Automobile Association Photographs; BKS Aerial Photographs; Buildings of Ireland Photographs; Alec R. Day ARPS Collection; J.V. Downes Slide Collection; Kieran Glendining Collection; Green Studio Collection; Thomas Gunn Collection; Paddy Healy Photographs; Westropp Albums; as well as on-going photographic survey work carried out by the IAA.

88   Irish Capuchin Archives

Address	Capuchin Friary Church Street Dublin 7
Telephone	(056) 21439
Fax	(056) 22025
E-mail	bencullen@eircom.net
Enquiries to	Revd Dr Benedict Cullen OFM Cap Archivist Capuchin Friary Friary Street Kilkenny
Opening hours and facilities	Access by prior arrangement only

Major collections

Administrative documents and correspondence of the Irish province, 1885–1970.

Material relating to the history of the Irish Capuchin province, 1633–.

89   Irish Christian Brothers St Mary's Provincialate

Address	Christian Brothers' Provincialate 274 North Circular Road Dublin 7
Telephone	(01) 868 0247
Fax	(01) 838 1075
E-mail	cbprov@tinet.ie
Enquiries to	The Archivist or Revd Brother Provincial
Opening hours and facilities	Postal enquiry; photocopying

Major collections
Material relating to the history, evolution and administration of the Congregation. Material relating to St Mary's province, 1956–.

90   Irish Christian Brothers St Helen's Provincialate

Address	York Road Dún Laoghaire County Dublin
Telephone	(01) 280 1214/284 1656
Fax	(01) 284 1657
E-mail	yorkroad@indigo.ie
Enquiries to	The Archivist
Opening hours	10.00–3.30, Mon–Fri, excluding Holy days; appointment necessary

Major collections
Annals of Christian Brothers' discontinued establishments from throughout the country. Minutes of Provincial Chapters. Registers of postulants, novices and industrial schools. Minutes of the Christian Brothers' Education Committee.

Material relating to the life and work of Br Edmund Ignatius Rice and the early brothers.

Collection of historical and educational publications including Christian Brothers' publications; Reports of the Commissioners of Inquiry into Irish Education (1827); and correspondence concerning the Erasmus Smith Schools Act Scheme, 1941.

91   Irish Film Archive
Film Institute of Ireland

Address	6 Eustace Street Dublin 2
Telephone	(01) 679 5744
Fax	(01) 677 8755
E-mail	archive@ifc.ie
Website	www.fii.ie
Enquiries to	The Archive Curator
Opening hours and facilities	film and tape: 10.00–1.00, 2.00–5.00, Mon–Fri; appointment necessary; scale of charges on application; paper archives: 10.00–1.00, Mon–Fri; appointment necessary; reference library: 2.00–5.30, Mon–Fri, 2.00–7.00 Wed; no appointment necessary; photocopying

Major collections

The film collection numbers over 15,000 cans, acquired by donation from public and private bodies, reflecting the history of professional and amateur film production in Ireland from 1897.

Much of the film collection has been transferred to videotape for reference purposes, the tape collection now amounting to over 1,000 VHS tapes of Irish material.

The paper archives collection includes stills, posters and other documents relating to Irish cinema.

The Tiernan McBride Library contains over 1,200 books, film periodicals and film-related CD ROMs on all aspects of national and international cinema. A cuttings file on Irish film production is also maintained.

92   Irish Huguenot Archive

Address   Representative Church Body Library
Braemor Park
Churchtown
Dublin 14

Telephone   (01) 492 3979

Fax   (01) 492 4770

E-mail   rcblibrarian@ireland.anglican.org

Enquiries to   The Honorary Curator

Opening hours   9.00–1.00, 2.00–5.00, Mon–Fri
and facilities

Major collections

Pedigrees and papers of Huguenot families, especially Rambaut, Hauntenville, Robinette, Fleury, Gaussen, Le Bas, De Brecquet.

Papers relating to the Huguenot cemeteries in Dublin, 1960s–80s.

Addresses at the annual Huguenot service in St Patrick's Cathedral, Dublin, 1987–.

Newsletters of the Irish Section of the Huguenot Society.

93   Irish Jesuit Archives

Address   35 Lower Leeson Street
Dublin 2

Telephone   (01) 676 1099

Fax   (01) 676 2984

E-mail   archives@s–j.ie

Enquiries to   The Archivist

Opening hours   By appointment
and facilities

Guides   Fergus O'Donoghue SJ, 'Irish Jesuit archives', *Archivium Hibernicum* 41 (1986), 64–71; Stephen Redmond SJ, 'A guide to the Irish Jesuit Province archives' *Archivium Hibernicum* 50 (1996), 127–31

Major collections
Administrative and pastoral material, including correspondence with the Jesuit
  generalate; papers of noted Jesuits; papers relating to property; manuscripts
  of books and sermons; retreat notes; manuscripts in Irish; photographs; papers
  relating to Irish Jesuit missions in Australia, the Far East and Zambia. Original
  manuscripts cover the period, 1575–1970, transcripts, 1540–1774.

94   Irish Jewish Museum

Address	3/4 Walworth Road
	South Circular Road
	Dublin 8
Telephone	(01) 453 1797/490 1857
Enquiries to	The Curator
Opening hours and facilities	11.00–3.30, Sun, Tue, Thur, May–Sept; 10.30–2.30, Sun only, Oct–Apr; other times by appointment

Major collections
Minute books and records of various communal institutions and synagogues,
  registers of births, marriages and deaths, correspondence and communal
  publications, 1820–.

95   Irish Labour History Society Museum and Archives

Address	Beggar's Bush
	Haddington Road
	Dublin 4
Telephone	(01) 873 5879
E-mail	peopcoll@iol.ie
Website	www.ilhsonline.org
Enquiries to	ILHS Secretary, Fionnuala Richardson
	People's College, Parnell Square, Dublin 1
Opening hours and facilities	10.00–1.00, Tue, Wed, Thur; other times by appointment

Guides	Summary descriptions of collections acquired by the ILHS and deposited in University College Dublin Archives Department (q.v.) or held in the ILHS Museum and Archives are published in *Saothar*, the Society's journal, 5–27 (1979–2002); the journal also includes guides to collections of labour interest in other repositories, both in Ireland and abroad.

Major collections

Postal and Telecommunications Workers' Union (merged with the Communications Union of Ireland in 1989 to form the Communication Workers' Union): rule books and annual conference reports; branch records; material relating to the Union's involvement with ITUC/ICTU, the Labour Party and international bodies; publications of other postal workers' unions.

Papers of William Norton (1900–63) relating to all aspects of Norton's public life as general secretary of the POWU, Labour Party TD for Kildare, 1932–62, leader of the Labour Party, 1932–60, Tánaiste and Minister for Social Welfare, 1948–52, and Minister for Industry and Commerce, 1954–7.

Irish Women Workers' Union: minute books and annual reports; records relating to the union's representation of laundry and print workers and its participation in the national trade union movement and the Labour Party, 1917–84.

Workers' Union of Ireland records, 1924–89: includes administrative and branch records, mainly late 1940s–, and including some papers of James Larkin Jnr.

Association of Secondary Teachers of Ireland: organisational and branch records including material on educational policy, 1919–94.

Some private paper collections including papers of Cathal O'Shannon.

96   Irish Land Commission, Records Branch

Address	National Archives Building Bishop Street Dublin 8
Telephone	(01) 475 0766
Fax	(01) 478 5857
E-mail	john.dunne@agriculture.gov.ie

Enquiries to	The Keeper of Records
Opening hours and facilities	10.00–12.30, 2.30–4.30, Mon–Fri; by appointment only. Limited access and photocopying in accordance with Land Commission Rules

Major collections

The largest series of records held by the Land Commission Records Branch are the title documents and ancillary papers pertaining to estates acquired by both the Land Commission and the Congested Districts Board under different Land Acts since 1881. As well as deeds dating from the 17th century these include abstracts of title, maps lodged by vendors of estates, schedules of particulars of tenancies, orders vesting estates in the Land Commission, schedules of particulars of the allocation of the estate purchase moneys, tenants' fiated purchase agreements and resale maps. Other record series created under the auspices of the numerous administrative branches of the Land Commission include the following: Irish Land Commission Minute Books, 1892–1918; Fair Rent Orders and Agreements, 1881–1920; Apportionment Orders, Right of Way Orders and other Orders of the Judicial Commissioners, 1881–; Registers of Affidavits, 1881–1974; Secretariat files, 1881–1985; Originating Statements by Landlords, 1892–1904; Final Schedules of Incumbrances, 1886–1951; Land Purchase Department Records of Proceedings, 1885–1955. Records of the Church Temporalities Commission includes leases of Church property, *c.*1600–1869; mortgages, conveyances and grants in perpetuity, 1869–*c.*1880; records relating to Tithe Rent Charge, 1869–1973; Commutation Claims, 1870–2; Applotment Books, 1872; Investigators' Reports, 1869–79; Seal Books, 1908–27; glebe maps, 1835–77.

97   Irish Linen Centre & Lisburn Museum

Address	Market Square Lisburn BT28 1AG
Telephone	(02892) 663377
Fax	(02892) 672624
E-mail	irishlinencentre@lisburn.gov.uk
Enquiries to	The Research Officer
Opening hours and facilities	9.30–4.30, Mon–Fri; appointment necessary; photocopying; microfilm reader/printer

Major collections

The library and archives of the former Lambeg Industrial Research Association (LIRA) includes books, journals, pamphlets and ephemera, 18th–20th centuries; together with the administrative records of the organisation from its foundation in the 1920s until its closure in 1993.

Manuscript material and maps relating to Lisburn and the Lagan Valley.

Photographic collection.

The Reference Library houses a collection of 2,000 books and journals; copies of local newspapers; and microfilm copies of census schedules for Lisburn and district.

98   Irish Railway Record Society

Address	Heuston Station Dublin 8
Telephone	(028) 9752 8428
Enquiries to	The Archivist
Opening hours and facilities	8.00–10.00, Tue; by appointment
Guides	Joseph Leckey, *The records of the Irish Transport Genealogical Archive.* Occasional Publication No. 7 of the Irish Railway Record Society (1985); Joseph Leckey and Peter Rigney, *IRRS Archival Collections D1–D10* (1976); Joseph Leckey, *The records of the County Donegal railways* (1980)

Major collections

Transport archives, 18th century–, including waterways, roads, and air transport, but predominantly railways. Private collections and non–current archives of CIÉ, the national transport undertaking, and its constituent companies.

Incorporates Irish Transport Genealogical Archive: the personal records of transport employees, 1870s–1950s as far as these have been located. Fine collection of transport and other directories.

Ordnance Survey maps covering much of the railway system, with 5,000 other maps and drawings.

Most complete collection of parliamentary plans of Irish railways outside the House of Lords Record Office. Other books of plans include docks, drainage, tramways, reservoirs, markets, and hotels as well as contractors' plans of railways.

99   Irish Room, North Eastern Education and Library Board

Address	County Hall
	Castlerock Road
	Coleraine
	County Londonderry BT1 3HP
	Northern Ireland
Telephone	(02870) 351026
Fax	(02870) 351247
E-mail	elvacooper@hotmail.com
Website	www.neelb.org.uk
Enquiries to	Group Librarian, Coleraine Group
Opening hours and facilities	10.00–12.00, 1.30–4.30, Mon–Fri; at other times by appointment; photocopying, microfilom reader-printer

Major collections

Local studies collection focusing on the history of Coleraine and the surrounding area includes local newspapers, pamphlets, maps and photographs; and copies of census and valuation records of local interest.

Papers of Dr Hugh Mullin, local historian, including manuscripts and notebooks.

100   Irish Rugby Football Union

Address	62 Lansdowne Road
	Dublin 4
Telephone	(01) 647 3800
Fax	(01) 647 3801
Website address	www.irfu.ie
Enquiries to	The Chief Executive
Opening hours and facilities	By appointment; photocopying

Major collections

Minute books, miscellaneous papers, photographs, press cuttings, memorabilia, 1874–.

101   Irish Theatre Archive

Address   Dublin City Library and Archive
                  138–142 Pearse Street
                  Dublin 2

Telephone   (01) 674 4800

Fax   (01) 674 4881

E-mail   cityarchives@dublincity.ie

Website   www.dublincity.ie

Enquiries to   The Honorary Archivist

Opening hours   10.00–8.00, Mon–Thur; 10.00–5.00, Fri–Sat;
and facilities photocopying; photography

Guides   Articles in *Prompts: Bulletin of the Irish Theatre Arch-*
                  ive, nos. 1–6

Major collections

Archives of major theatres including An Damer; Cork Theatre Company;
Dublin Masque Theatre Guild; Dublin Theatre Festival; Gaiety Theatre,
Dublin; Irish Theatre Company; Olympia Theatre, Dublin; Rough Magic
Theatre Company; Brendan Smith Academy; and Theatre Royal, Dublin.
Private papers of players and designers including P.J. Bourke; Eddie Cooke;
Ursula Doyle; Donald Finlay; James N. Healy; Eddie Johnston; Nora
Lever; Mícheál Mac Liammóir; Dennis Noble; Jimmy O'Dea; Shelah
Richards; and Cecil Sheridan.
Extensive collection of programmes, posters, photographs, press cuttings,
prompt–books, costume and stage designs relating to theatres, amateur
groups and theatre clubs; together with original plays in typescript and
manuscript.

102   Irish Traditional Music Archive/ Taisce Ceoil Dúchais Éireann

Address   63 Merrion Square
                  Dublin 2

Telephone   (01) 661 9699

Fax   (01) 662 4585

Website address	www.itma.ie
Enquiries to	The Secretary
Opening hours and facilities	10.00–1.00, 2.0–5.00, Mon–Fri; photocopying; photography
Guides	Nicholas Carolan, *Irish Traditional Music Archive/ Taisce Cheol Dúchais Éireann: the first ten years/ na chéad deich mbliana (1997)*; Hugh Shields (ed.), *Tunes of the Munster pipers: Irish traditional music from the James Goodman manuscripts* (1998); Colette Moloney, *The Irish music manuscripts of Edward Bunting (1773–1843): an introduction and catalogue* (2000); information leaflets available on request

Major collections

Over 18,000 hours of sound recordings, 1890s–: commercial 78s, SPs, EPs, LPs, audio cassettes and CDs. Field sound recordings on cylinders, reel–to–reel tapes, audio cassettes, DAT, mini discs and CDs, include the Breathnach, Shields, Hamilton, Ó Conluain, Carroll–Mackenzie, MacWeeney, de Buitléar, RTÉ and BBC Radio collections, 20th century.

Printed matter: over 18,000 works of reference, serials, song and instrumental collections, studies, sheet music, ballad sheets, programmes and ephemera including posters, flyers and newspaper cuttings, 18th century–.

More than 6,000 photographic and other images, 19th century–.

Music manuscripts, theses and other unpublished material, 18th century–.

Over 1,000 video recordings, 20th century–.

103   Jesus and Mary Sisters (Congregation of the Religious of Jesus and Mary)

Address	Convent of Jesus and Mary Our Lady's Grove Goatstown Road Dublin 14
Telephone	(01) 298 4569
Fax	(01) 296 3793
E-mail	amclough@gofree.indigo.ie
Enquiries to	The Archivist

| *Opening hours* | By appointment; |
| *and facilities* | photocopying |

Major collections
Archives of the congregation in the Irish Province including correspondence
with higher superiors and material relating to the ministry of Irish Sisters
in other provinces of the congregation.

104 James Joyce Museum

Address	Joyce Tower
	Sandycove
	County Dublin
Telephone	(01) 280 9265
Fax	(01) 280 9265
E-mail	joycetower@dublintourism.ie
Website	www.visitdublin.com
Enquiries to	The Curator
Opening hours	10.00–1.00, 2.00–5.00, Mon–Sat, 2.00–6.00, Sun. and
and facilities	public holidays, Apr–Oct; by arrangement, Nov–Mar,
	contact the Dublin Writers Museum (q.v.)

Major collections
Letters and papers, portraits, photographs, first and rare editions, printed
ephemera and personal possessions of James Joyce (1882–1941), including his death mask, guitar, waistcoat and cabin trunk.

105 The John F. Kennedy Arboretum
Dúchas The Heritage Service

Address	New Ross
	County Wexford
Telephone	(051) 388171
Fax	(051) 388172
E-mail	jfkarboretum@duchas.ie

Website	www.heritageireland.ie
Enquiries to	The Director
Opening hours and facilities	10.00–8.00, May–Aug; 10.00–6.30, Apr–Sept; 10.00–5.00, Oct–Mar

Major collections

Records for each specimen in the arboretum, which contains 4,500 taxa, including height, stem diameter and crown spread, 1968–1989 .

Records of species in 200 forest plots including height, basal area and volume, 1966–95.

106   Kerry County Library

Address	Local History and Archives Kerry County Library Moyderwell Tralee County Kerry
Telephone	(066) 712 1200
Fax	(066) 712 9202
Email	archivist@kerrycolib.ie
Enquiries to	The Archivist
Opening hours and facilities	Local History: 10.00–1.00, 2.00–5.00, Mon–Sat; Archives: by appointment. photocopying, microfilm reader/printers.

Major collections

Board of Guardians minute books: Cahirciveen, 1905–22; Dingle, 1840–1920; Glin, 1870–91; Kenmare, 1840–1921; Killarney, 1840–1923; Listowel, 1845–1922; Tralee, 1845–1922; rough minute books: Dingle, 1849–1921; Killarney, 1840–71; Listowel, 1856–99; Tralee, 1845–1922.

Rural District Council minute books: Cahirciveen, 1900–25; Dingle, 1899–1925; Kenmare, 1899–1921; Killarney, 1900–25; Listowel, 1900–11; Tralee, 1900–25.

Kerry Board of Health minute books: Board of Health, 1925–31; Board of Health and Public Assistance, 1930–42; Board of Health and Labourers' Acts, 1937–42; Board of Health (TB Section), 1927–31; Board of Health and Public Assistance (TB Section), 1932–42.

Kerry County Committee of Agriculture minute books, 1920–88.
Kerry Field Club: minute books, 1939–57; correspondence and accounts, 1940–57.
The Kerryman photographic archive, 1957–88.

107   Kerry Diocesan Archives

Address	Bishop's House
	Killarney
	County Kerry
Telephone	(064) 31168
Fax	(064) 31364
E-mail	bishopshouse@eircom.net
Website	dioceseofkerry.ie
Enquiries to	The Archivist
Opening hours and facilities	By appointment

Major collections
Material connected with episcopates of Nicholas Madgett, bishop of Kerry (1753–74), and of each subsequent bishop of the diocese, as well as more personal papers of several bishops and some priests.

108   Kildare County Library Local Studies Department

Address	History and Family Research Centre
	Riverbank
	Main Street
	Newbridge
	County Kildare
Telephone	(045) 432690
Fax	(045) 431611

E-mail	localhistory@kildarecoco.ie
Enquiries to	The Librarian, Local Studies Department
Opening hours and facilities	Tue-Sat, by appointment; photocopying, microfilm reader/printers, scanning, digital photography

Major collections

Shackleton/Leadbeater collection: letters, poems and books relating to the Shackleton family of Ballitore, late 18th–early 19th century.

Teresa Brayton collection: poems, short stories, letters, photographs and memorabilia relating to Teresa Brayton, author of *The old bog road,* 1868–1943.

Verschoyle estate, Counties Dublin and Kildare: rentals and other papers, 1841–77.

Extensive reference library of local newspapers and journals; and microform and published editions of census, valuation, survey and folklore collections.

109   Kildare & Leighlin Diocesan Archives

Address	Bishop's House Carlow
Telephone	(059) 917 6725
Fax	(059) 917 6850
E-mail	chancellorkandl@eircom.net
Website	www.dioceseofkildareandleighlinn.ie
Enquiries to	The Diocesan Chancellor
Opening hours and facilities	By arrangement with the Diocesan Chancellor; application in writing

Major collections

Papers of bishops, 1745–1968. Some collections relating to clergy. Parish returns and vicars' visitation papers. Accounts, notebooks, and sermon manuscripts.

110   Kilkenny Archaeological Society

Address	Rothe House
	Kilkenny
Telephone	(056) 22893
Fax	(056) 22893
E-mail	rothehouse@eircom.net
Website	www.irishroots.net/kilknny.htm
Enquiries to	The Librarian
Opening hours and facilities	2.30–4.30, 7.30–9.30, Tue; 2.30–4.30, Wed; at other times by arrangement

Major collections

Langrishe Papers, Knocktopher Abbey, County Kilkenny, 1667–1923: estate records, family correspondence, wills, maps, surveys, rent records and leases.

Buggy & Co., solicitors, Kilkenny: legal papers relating to numerous Kilkenny families, *c.*1823–1940.

Collections of legal documents including wills, probate records, marriage settlements, leases, mortgages, affidavits, and correspondence, including some papers of Wheeler-Cuffe, Lyrath, Kilkenny, and Mrs Montague, Kilferagh, *c.*1706–1945.

Local newspaper reference collection, 18th–20th centuries.

Research files on various notable local families including the Rothes, Langtons, Andersons and Crottys. Register of Kilkenny World War 1 combatants.

111   Kilkenny Borough Council

Address	City Hall
	High Street
	Kilkenny
Telephone	(056) 21076
Fax	(056) 63422

Enquiries to	The Town Clerk
E-mail	dobrien@kilkennycoco.ie
Opening hours and facilities	By appointment or postal enquiry; photocopying

Major collections

Charters, grants, letters patent of the city of Kilkenny, 1170–1862, including the 1st charter of William earl of Pembroke to the burgesses of Kilkenny, 1170, and the charter of James I, 1609, creating Kilkenny a city. Minute books of the Corporation, including the first minute book, the 'Liber Primus Kilkennienses', 1231–1538; minutes of the 'Mayor and Citizens' of Kilkenny, 1656–1843; minutes of the 'Mayor Aldermen and Burgesses', 1843–1952; minutes of various committee meetings, 1892–1938; proceedings of the Corporation of Irishtown, 1544–1834; minutes of the Kilkenny Urban Sanitary Authority, 1875–6, 1917–42. Grand Roll of Freemen of the city of Kilkenny, 1760–. Deeds, conveyances, leases, letters, petitions and addresses, *c.*13th–19th century.

112   Kilkenny County Library

Address	6 Rose Inn Street NIB Building Kilkenny
Telephone	(056) 91160
Fax	(056) 91168
E-mail	katlibs@iol.ie
Enquiries to	The Assistant Librarian
Opening hours and facilities	10.30–1.00, 2.00–5.00, Mon–Fri; photocopying

Major collections

Local administrative records including Board of Guardian records, 1839–1923; Rural District Council records, 1894–1926; Grand Jury records, 1838–98; Registers of Electors, 1896–1994.

Records of Kilkenny County Council including Committee of Agriculture, 1924–41, County Board of Health, 1922–42, County Library Committee, 1910–, County Council minute books, 1899–1990, County Manager's orders, 1942–, valuation lists, rent and rate books and general files from various Council departments.

Callan Corporation indentures, 1720–1819, and Callan Town Commissioners administrative records, 1897–1944.

Private collections include indentures, wills and mortages, 1760–1924; Kilkenny City business records, early 20th century; records of Theatre Unlimited in Kilkenny, 1985–6; Arts Week records, 1974–86; and business records of Clover Meats, Waterford, 1920–80.

Photographic collections including the Lawrence, Valentine, and Seymore Crawford collections; Bolton Street College of Technology Architectural Faculty amenity study photographs, 1970; Bord Fáilte collection; industrial archaeology survey of County Kilkenny; and various collections of photographs of locations and activities in the city and county, early 20th century.

113   Killaloe Diocesan Archives

Address	Westbourne Ennis County Clare
Telephone	(065) 682 8638
Fax	(065) 684 2538
Enquiries to	The Diocesan Secretary
Opening hours and facilities	By appointment or postal enquiry; photocopying

Major collections

Notebooks of Canon John Clancy: mainly extracts from 19th-century newspapers.

Parish notes: files for each parish consisting mainly of returns to a questionnaire relating to antiquities, folklore and churches, prepared by Dermot F. Gleeson in the early 1940s.

Material on microfilm relating to Killaloe from the Congregation de Propaganda Fide in Rome, 1620–1900.

Notebooks, manuscripts and books of Monsignor Ignatius Murphy.

114   Kilmainham Gaol Museum

Address	Inchicore Road Dublin 8
Telephone	(01) 453 5984
Fax	(01) 453 2037
E-mail	kilmainhamgaol@duchas.ie
Enquiries to	The Curator
Opening hours and facilities	9.30–6.00, Mon–Sat, Apr–Sep; 9.30–5.30, Mon–Sat, Oct–Mar;10.00–6.00, Sun; access to archives by appointment only

Major collections

A miscellaneous collection of documents, photographs, uniforms, arms and personal effects, 1798–1924, with particularly interesting material from the 1916–23 period.

115   Kilmore Diocesan Archives

Address	Bishop's House Cullies Cavan
Telephone	(049) 4331496
E-mail	diocesansecretary@kilmorediocese.ie
Website	www.kilmorediocese.ie
Enquiries to	The Diocesan Archivist
Opening hours and facilities	By appointment

Major collections

Correspondence and papers of bishops including Lenten pastorals, letters to Rome, private office papers, sermons, visitation books, deeds, plans, wills, photographs and press cuttings, 1836–.

Correspondence and papers of priests of the diocese including the collections of Owen F. Traynor, T.P. Cunningham and Dr Philip O'Connell, the diocesan historian.

116   Kilrush Town Council and Kilrush (Cappa Pier) Harbour Authority

Address	Town Hall Kilrush County Clare
Telephone	(065) 905 1047/905 1596
Fax	(065) 905 2821
E-mail	kilrush@clarecoco.ie
Website	www.kilrush.ie
Enquiries to	The Town Clerk
Opening hours and facilities	9.30–4.00, Mon–Fri; photocopying

Major collections

Minute books, 1885–; harbour arrivals and departures books, 1875–; general maintenance and wages ledgers and printed abstracts of accounts, 1885–.

117   The King's Hospital

Address	Palmerstown Dublin 20
Telephone	(01) 626 5933
Fax	(01) 623 0349
E-mail	kingshos@iol.ie
Enquiries to	The Archivist
Opening hours and facilities	By appointment;
Guides	Brief listing in Lesley Whiteside, *A history of the King's Hospital, Dublin* (2nd ed., Dublin, 1985)

Major collections

Records relating to the school: annual accounts, 1669–76, 1771–1809, 1858–; building accounts, 1669–75, 1742–45; partial accounts for the building of Blackhall Place, 1773–4; board minutes, 1674–1746, 1779–1829, 1841–; general committee minutes, 1798–1823, 1829–; headmasters' reports, 1884–; lists of pupils, some incomplete, 1675–1867, 1895–; memorials for admission, 1890–1940; fee registers, 1908; reminiscences of past pupils; records relating to the sporting history of the school, 1890–, including a large collection of photographs.

Records relating to property: rentals and rent ledgers, 1669–83, 1730–79, 1794–; maps of estates in Dublin and Tipperary; deeds.

Records of Mercer's School, Castleknock, County Dublin: board minutes, 1832–1968; accounts and rent rolls, 1738–1822; accounts, 1864–1901; lists of pupils, 1865–; deeds of property in Dublin; small collection of photographs.

Records of Morgan's School, Castleknock, County Dublin: board minutes, 1909–58; takeover papers; deeds.

Oral history collection of past pupils and staff; small collection of videos.

118   King's Inns (The Honorable Society of King's Inns)

Address	Henrietta Street Dublin 1
Telephone	(01) 878 2119
Fax	(01) 874 4846
E-mail	library@kingsinns.ie
Website address	www.kingsinns.ie
Enquiries to	The Librarian
Opening hours and facilities	10.00–8.30, Mon–Thur; 10.30–6.00, Fri; I 0.00– 1.00, Sat; outside the academic year Library opens 10.00–5.00, Mon–Fri; researchers should write in advance stating the nature of their enquiry; photocopying
Guides	Julitta Clancy, *Records of the Honourable Society of King's Inns: guide and descriptive lists* (in–house production, 1989); Nigel Cochrane, 'The archives and manuscripts of the King's Inns Library', *Irish Archives* 1 (1989), 25–30; Pádraig de Brún, *Catalogue of Irish manuscripts in King's Inns Library Dublin* (Dublin Institute

for Advanced Studies, 1972); Edward Keane, P. Beryl
Phair and Thomas U. Sadleir (eds), *King's Inns admission papers, 1607–1867* (Dublin, Irish Manuscripts
Commission, 1982); Colum Kenny, 'The records of
King's Inns, Dublin', in Daire Hogan and W.N.
Osborough (eds), *Brehons, serjeants and attorneys*
(Dublin, Irish Academic Press & Irish Legal History
Society, 1990), 231–48; T. Power, 'The "Black Book"
of King's Inn: an introduction with an abstract of contents', *Irish Jurist* 20 (1985), 135–312; Wanda Ryan-Smolin, *King's Inns portraits* (Dublin, The Council of
King's Inns, 1992); John Montague, *King's Inns portrait
prints and drawings* (in-house production, 2000)

Major collections
Archives of the Society, 1607–1917, which include the 'Black Book'
1607–1730, Bench Minutes, 1792–1917, admission records of barristers
and admission records of attorneys up to 1866.
29 Irish language manuscripts, the majority dating from the 18th century,
but five of which were written as early as the 15th century.
Private paper collection of John Patrick Prendergast (1808–93).
Manuscripts of Bartholomew Thomas Duhigg (*c.*1750–1813), Assistant
Librarian to the Society.
Manuscript parliamentary journals and miscellaneous legal manuscripts.

119   Kinsale Harbour Commissioners

Address	Harbour Office
	Custom's Quay
	Kinsale
	County Cork
Telephone	(021) 477 2503
Fax	(021) 477 4695
E-mail	kharbour@iol.ie
Website	www.kinsaleharbour.com
Enquiries to	The Harbour Master
Opening hours and facilities	By appointment

Major collections
Minute books, 1870–; arrivals and departures books, 1898–; export and
  import books, 1898–; maps, plans and drawings of the harbour, 1883;
  cash books, 1879–; bye-laws, 1870–.

120 The Labour Party

Address	17 Ely Place
	Dublin 2
Telephone	(01) 678 4700
Fax	(01) 661 2640
E-mail	mike_allen@labour.ie
Website address	www.labour.ie
Enquiries to	General Secretary
Opening hours and facilities	9.30–4.30, Mon–Fri; photocopying

Major collections
Records of the parliamentary party, 1970–; records of the party adminis-
  tration, 1970s–.
Annual reports, 1912–.

121 Land Registry

Address	Central Office
	Chancery Street
	Dublin 7
Telephone	(01) 670 7500
Fax	(01) 804 8144
E-mail	webmaster@landregistry.ie
Website address	www.landregistry.ie
Enquiries to	The Chief Executive/Registrar of Deeds and Titles
Opening hours and facilities	10.30–4.30, Mon–Fri; photocopying; microfilming, digitising

Major collections

Folio Series: each folio contains a description of a particular holding, the
name, address and description of the owner and details of any burden or
charges affecting the property, 1892–.

Land Registry Maps: each map contains plans drawn of each holding indi-
cating the position and boundaries of the property the ownership of which
has been registered, 1892–.

122   Laois County Library

Address	County Hall
	Portlaoise
Telephone	(0502) 64000
Fax	(0502) 22313
Enquiries to	The County Librarian
Opening hours	9.00–5.00, Mon–Fri; by appointment;
and facilities	photocopying

Major collections

Boards of Guardians minute books: Abbeyleix Union, 1844–1919;
Mountmellick Union, 1845–1920; Donaghmore Union, 1851–86.

Durrow Dispensary minute book, 1880–98.

Grand Jury presentment book, Stradbally summer assizes, 1816–42.

Urban District Council minute books: Abbeyleix, 1909–25; Athy, 1913–25;
Cloneygowan, 1903–23; Mountmellick, 1899–1926; Roscrea, 1905–17;
Slievemargy, 1909–25.

Queen's County/Laois County Council records: minute books, 1899–2002;
rate books, 1934–70; account books, 1927–37; Barrow drainage scheme
rate books, 1939–46; blind welfare scheme, 1934–52; free milk distrib-
ution scheme, 1942–50; tuberculosis committee minute books, 1915–25;
road works, 1929–30; Manager's Orders, 1946–2002; financial statement
books, 1920–48; labourers' cottages ledgers, 1884–1947; minute book
and correspondence of Portlaoise swimming pool, 1967–76.

Laois County Committee of Agriculture minute books, 1905–87.

Rural district council records: Mountmellick minute books, 1899–1920,
rough minute books, 1899–1903, letter books, 1915–26; Abbeyleix general ledgers, 1909–25, labourers' cottages general rentals, 1909–25;

Cloneygowan minute books, 1903–18, Labourers' Acts minutes, 1908–18; Athy No. 2 minute book, 1913–14, labourers' cottages general rental, 1923–25; Slievemargy minute books, 1923–25, general ledgers, 1909–25; Roscrea No. 3 ledgers, 1905–17.

Hospital records: register of cases sent to external hospitals, 1926–58; home assistance, 1934–53; hospital administration records for County Infirmary, 1880–1924; County Hospital, 1933–60; County Home, 1933–4; Abbeyleix District Hospital, 1924–53; St Brigid's Sanitorium, Shaen, 1930–61.

Board of Health records, 1907–60; Public Assistance minute books, 1924–40.

Bye-laws of Maryborough, 1731; tenants' account book, Deerpark, Kilkenny, 1836–46; Stradbally Petty Sessions order books, 1851–96; Trustees of River Nore Drainage minute book, 1855–1939, and account books, 1855–1945; Maryborough Lawn Tennis & Croquet Club minute book, 1914–31.

Milltown estate papers, 1820–70.

123   Ledwidge Museum

Address	Jeanville
	Slane
	County Meath
Telephone	(041) 98 24544
Enquiries to	The Secretary
Opening hours	10.00–1.00, 2.00–6.00, Sun–Sat, summer;
and facilities	10.00–1.00, 2.00–4.30, Sun–Sat, winter
Guides	General information leaflet

Major collections
Manuscript poems, correspondence and memorabilia of the poet Frances Ledwidge, 1887–1917.

124   Leitrim County Library

Address	Ballinamore
	County Leitrim
Telephone	(078) 44012

Fax	(078) 44425
E-mail	leitrimlibrary@eircom.net
Enquiries to	Leabharlannaí Contae
Opening hours and facilities	10.00–1.00, 2.00–5.00, Mon–Fri; photocopying

Major collections

Mohill Board of Guardians minute books, 1839–1922; Manorhamilton Board of Guardians minute books, 1839–1923; Carrick-on-Shannon Board of Guardians minute books, 1843–1919.

Records of Kinlough Rural District Council, 1902–25; Mohill Rural District Council, 1899–1924; Manorhamilton Rural District Council, 1899–1925.

Court records.

Estate papers from some Leitrim estates.

Large collection of ledgers and account books from various shops and business premises.

Minute books of various committees.

125 Lifford Old Courthouse

Address	The Diamond Lifford County Donegal
Telephone	(074) 41733
Fax	(074) 41228
E-mail	seatofpower@eircom.net
Website address	www.infowing.ie/seatofpower
Enquiries to	The Manager
Opening hours and facilities	9.00–4.30, Mon–Fri, 12.30–4.30, Sun; by appointment.

Major collections

Rupert Coughlan collection of documents, manuscripts and charts of the O'Donnell family and chieftains.

Letters and photographs relating to the Old Courthouse and Gaol.

126 Limerick Diocesan Archives

Address	Diocesan Office 6 O'Connell Street Limerick
Telephone	(061) 315856
Fax	(061) 310186
E-mail	diocoff@eircom.net
Website address	www.limerickdiocese heritage.org
Enquiries to	The Diocesan Secretary
Opening hours and facilities	Permission must be sought to consult diocesan archives available on microfilm in the National Library of Ireland (q.v.)

Major collections
Records on microfilm in the National Library include baptismal and marriage records of the parishes of the diocese to 1900.
Material held in the diocesan archives includes the 14th-century Black Book of Limerick.

127 Limerick Museum

Address	Castle Lane Nicholas Street Limerick
Telephone	(061) 417826
E-mail	lwalsh@limerickcity.ie
Website address	www.limerickcity.ie
Enquiries to	The Curator
Opening hours and facilities	10.00–1.00, 2.15–5.00, Tue–Sat; Curator available Mon–Fri, by appointment; photocopying; photography

Major collections
Miscellaneous documents, maps and photographs relating to Limerick, c.17th century–.

128   Limerick Archives

Address   The Granary
Michael Street
Limerick

Telephone   (061) 415125

Fax   (061) 312985

Enquiries to   The Archivist

Opening hours   9.30–1.00, 2.15–5.30, Mon–Fri, by appointment;
and facilities   photocopying; microfilming

Major collections

Poor Law minute books, 1838–1923, and Rural District Council minute books, 1899–1925, for County Limerick.

Limerick County Council minute books, 1898–; County Board of Health minute books, 1923–44.

Limerick Corporation: freedom records, 1737–1905; Council and Committee minute books: 1841–; Tholsel Court records, 1773–1833.

Commissioners for St Michael's parish: minute books, 1819–44; rate books, 1811–44; night watch reports, 1833–49.

Limerick Chamber of Commerce: minute books, 1807–; export books, 1815–50.

Limerick Harbour Commissioners: minute books, pilot books, tonnage dues, 1823–.

Limerick House of Industry register, 1774–94.

St John's Hospital: minutes, correspondence, register of patients, accounts, 1816–1905.

Sir Vere Hunt papers, 1716–1818; Monteagle papers, 1605–1930; Coote papers, 1776–1843; miscellaneous deeds from solicitors' collections, 1624–1900.

129   Linen Hall Library

Address   17 Donegall Square North
Belfast BT1 5GD

Telephone   (02890) 321707

E-mail   info@linenhall.com

Website address   www.linenhall.com

Enquiries to   The Librarian

Opening hours   9.30–5.30, Mon–Fri; 9.30–4.00, Sat;
and facilities   photocopying

Major collections
Archives of the library, 1791–, including manuscript minutes of the
    Governors of the Library; wages books; minutes of various committees.
Manuscript meteorological records for Belfast, 1796–1906.
Joy MSS: selected materials for the annals of the province of Ulster, col-
    lected by Henry Joy, 18th century and early 19th century.
Minutes of the Belfast Literary Society, 1801–.
Minutes of Belfast Burns Society, 1931–.
Blackwood MSS: family history and pedigree collection compiled by
    R.W.H. Blackwood.
Belfast News Letter: index to births, marriages and deaths, 1738–1863.

130   Little Sisters of the Assumption

Address   Provincial House
    42 Rathfarnham Road
    Dublin 6W

Telephone   (01) 490 9850

Fax   (01) 492 5740

E-mail   lsa@indigo.ie

Enquiries to   The Secretary

Opening hours   9.00–5.00, Mon–Fri; appointment advisable;
and facilities   photocopying

Major collections
Material relating to the history of the Little Sisters of the Assumption in
    Ireland, containing information on founders, initial formation houses, and
    individual houses in Ireland, Wales and Ethiopia. Correspondence from
    the province to the motherhouse in Paris; General Chapter meetings; meet-
    ings in the province; and general correspondence.

131   Longford County Library

Address   County Library Headquarters
Annaly Carpark
Longford

Telephone   (043) 41124/5

Fax   (043) 41124/5

E-mail   longlib@iol.ie

Website address   www.longford.local.ie

Enquiries to   The County Librarian or Local Authority Archivist

Opening hours   9.30–1.00, 2.00–5.00, Mon–Thurs, 5.00 closing on Fri

Major collections

Grand Jury: abstracts of presentments, 1817–95.

Longford Poor Law Union: Board of Guardians minute books, 1839–1922.

Granard Poor Law Union: Board of Guardians minute books, 1855–1920.

Ballymahon Poor Law Union: Board of Guardians minute books, 1881–1921; return of Guardians and Officers, 1850–1919; return of admissions and births and deaths, 1858–1909; return of dispensaries, 1900–19.

Rural District Council minute books: Longford, 1892–1924; Granard No. 1, 1899–1925; Ballymahon, 1900–23; assorted material relating to labourers'cottages and other works.

County Council: quarterly minutes, 1922–26.

Labourers' Act minute books, 1886–96; County Register of Separate Charges, 1899–1925.

Longford Urban District Council minute books, 1897–1989, and related material.

Board of health and Public Assistance: minute books, 1926–41.

Drumlish Dispensary Committee: minute book, 1871–99.

Private collections include: Longford Militia regulations and record book, 1793–1855; Maria Edgeworth letters, 1815–49; estate records of the King-Harman family of Newcastle House, 1849–1949; rent books and account books of various estates including Newcomen, Kingston, Bole, West, Lorton, Fox and Shuldham, 19th century; papers of local historian, S.F. Ó Cianáin, 1910–40.

132   Loreto Sisters (Irish Branch of the Institute of the Blessed Virgin Mary)

Address	Central Archives 55 St Stephen's Green Dublin 2
Telephone	(01) 662 0158
Fax	(01) 662 0158
Website address	www.loreto.ie
Enquiries to	The Archivist
Opening hours and facilities	By appointment; photocopying

Major collections

Archives of the Irish branch of IBVM, 1822–.

Material relating to Mary Ward (1585–1645), foundress of IBVM and papers of Francis Teresa Ball (1794–1861), foundress of the Irish branch of IBVM, usually called Loreto.

Material relating to the administration of the Institute at Generalate and Provincial level.

Biographical material relating to individual members of the Institute.

133   Louth Local Authorities Archive Service

Address	Old Gaol Ardee Road Dundalk County Louth
Telephone	(042) 933 9387
Fax	(042) 933 9304
E-mail address	archive@louthcoco.ie
Enquiries to	The County Archivist
Opening hours and facilities	2.00–5.00, Mon, 9.30–1.00, Thurs, by appointment; photocopying

Major collections
Grand Jury records, 1815–99.
Board of Guardians records for Ardee, Drogheda and Dundalk, 1839–1924.
Rural District Council records for Ardee, Drogheda and Dundalk, 1899–1925.
Ardee Borough Court: court books, 1746–1917; minute book, 1889–1963.
Ardee Corporation: minute books, 1661–1841; survey, 1677; charters and property deeds, 17th–20th century; letter book, 1845–93.
Ardee Town Commissioners: minute books, financial records, letter books, 1843–1970.
Carlingford Corporation: minute book, 1694–1835.
Dundalk Borough Court: fines and committal books, 1855–1918.
Dundalk Town Commissioners: minute books, financial records, rate books, 1832–99.
Dundalk Urban District Council: minute books, maps, rate books, financial records, 1899–1970.
Dundalk Harbour Commissioners: minute books, arrival books, financial records, maps, *c.*1831–1976.
Dunleer Corporation: minute book, 1709–73.
Louth Agricultural Committee: minute books, 1901–85.
Louth County Council: minute, rate books, valuation books, financial records, engineering records, letter books, maps, miscellaneous material, 1899–1970.
Estate papers of Lord Louth, the earl of Roden, the earl of Carlingford, Edward O'Callaghan; papers of the Anglesey and Collon estates.
Family and personal papers of Caraher of Cardistown; Filgate of Lisrenny, Ardee; Hatch of Ardee; Kirwan of Castletown; Donaldson of Phipipstown; Fitzgerald of Fane Valley; Johnson of Lisdoo; Philips of Belcotton, Eastwood of Dundalk; Hinds of Dundalk.

134   Maritime Institute of Ireland

Address	Haigh Terrace Dun Laoghaire County Dublin
Telephone	(01) 280 0969
Enquiries to	The Honorary Secretary
Opening hours and facilities	By appointment; photocopying; photography

Major collections

Records of the Maritime Institute of Ireland: minutes of the Council, 1941–, and the Executive Committee, 1941–82; papers of the Honorary Research Officer, 1947–91; records of public meetings and other activities, 1941; minutes of the Museum Management Committee, 1978–.

Chart collection, photographic collection and press cuttings collection.

135   Archbishop Marsh's Library

Address	St Patrick's Close Dublin 8
Telephone	(01) 454 3511
Fax	(01) 454 3511
E-mail	keeper@marshlibrary.ie
Website address	www.marshlibrary.ie
Enquiries to	The Keeper
Opening hours and facilities	10.00–1.00, 2.00–5.00, Mon, Wed–Fri; 10.30–1.00, Sat
Guides	N.J.D. White, *Catalogue of the manuscripts remaining in Marsh's Library, Dublin* (1913); Muriel McCarthy, *Marsh's Library, Dublin* (2000)

Major collections

*c.*300 manuscripts from the collections of Narcissus Marsh (1638–1713), Archbishop of Armagh; Elie Bouhéreau (1643–1719), the first Keeper of the Library; and Dudley Loftus (1619–95), jurist and orientalist. The manuscripts, collected by Loftus and purchased by Archbishop Marsh, relate mainly to Irish history.

The manuscripts include a volume of the Lives of the Irish Saints, in Latin, dating from *c.*1400; a Sarum Processional from the Church of St John the Evangelist, Dublin, 15th century; and two volumes of Bishop Bedell's original translation of the Old Testament into Irish.

Collection of letters in French to Dr Bouhéreau, a Huguenot refugee, before he came to Ireland, 17th century.

Music manuscripts including 17th-century part books and a book of lute tabulature, late 16th century.

136   Mary Immaculate College

Address	South Circular Road Limerick
Telephone	(061) 314923
Fax	(061) 313632
E-mail	mary.brassil@mic.ul.ie
Enquiries to	The Librarian
Opening hours and facilities	9.00–10.00, during term time; 9.00–5.00, during vacations; photocopying

Major collections
Irish Folklore Commission collection.

137   Masonic Order (Grand Lodge of Ancient, Free & Accepted Masons of Ireland)

Address	Freemasons' Hall Molesworth Street Dublin 2
Telephone	(01) 676 1337/662 4485
Fax	(01) 662 5101
E-mail	library@freemason.ie
Website address	www.irish-freemasons.org
Enquiries to	The Librarian and Archivist
Opening hours and facilities	Mon–Fri; by appointment; photocopying; photography; microfilming

Major collections
Grand Lodge records: membership registers of 2,300 lodges and minute books of various administrative bodies. Correspondence files relating to Irish Masonic lodges at home and overseas, early 18th–20th century.
Subordinate Lodge records: minute books and other effects of individual lodges (*c.*300 individual collections).

Records of Masonic benevolent institutions including the records of the Masonic Female Orphan School (founded 1792) and the Masonic Boys' School (founded 1867). Charity Petitions, 18th–20th century. Restricted access.
Microfilms and photocopies of Irish Masonic records held in other custodies, 18th–20th century.

138 Mayo County Council

Address	Áras an Chontae The Mall Castlebar County Mayo
Telephone	(094) 24444
Fax	(094) 23937
E-mail	secretar@mayococo.ie
Website address	www.mayococo.ie
Enquiries to	The Archivist
Opening hours and facilities	9.00–1.00, 2.00–5.00; Mon–Fri; by appointment; photocopying

Major collections
Board of Guardians minutes: Swinford, 1883, 1893.
Poor Law archives: Ballinrobe, 1850–1919.
Rural District Council minutes: Castlebar, 1909–17, and Ballinrobe, 1903–25.
Urban District Council archives: Castlebar, 1901–, and Ballina, 1901–.
Mayo County Council archives including Council minutes, 1899–, and series from the various administrative sections of the Council, such as finance, housing, motor tax, roads and sanitary services, *c.* 1933–.
Papers of the Kenny family of Ballinrobe, 1730–1939.

139 Meath County Library

Address	Railway Street Navan County Meath
Telephone	(046) 21134/21451

E-mail	colibrar@meathcoco.ie
Enquiries to	The County Librarian
Opening hours and facilities	9.30–1.00, 2.00–5.00, Mon–Fri; 10.00–12.30, Sat; 7.00–8.30, Tue & Thur; photocopying

Major collections

Board of Guardians minute books: Dunshaughlin Union, 1839–1921; Kells Union, 1839–1922; Navan Union, 1839–1921; Oldcastle Union, 1870–1920; Trim Union, 1839–1921.

Rural District Council minute books: Kells, 1899–1923; Navan, 1899–1925; Dunshaughlin, 1899–1925; Ardee, 1899–1925; Edenderry, 1899–1917; Oldcastle, 1899–1917; Trim, 1899–1921.

Meath County Council: minutes, accounts, correspondence, valuation books, 1904–60.

Meath County Library Committee records, 1931–.

Meath County Infirmary, Navan, records, 1809–1960.

Board of Health: minute books 1934–42; Public Assistance record books, 1920–44.

Navan Urban District Council: minutes, accounts, correspondence, 1920–50.

Navan Town Commissioners: minutes, 1880–1902.

Trim Town Commissioners: minutes, accounts, 1895–1908.

Trim Urban District Council: minutes, accounts, rate books, 1927–50.

Kells Urban District Council: minutes, accounts, valuation books, committee minutes, 1897–1970.

Kells Town Commissioners: minutes, accounts, wages and expenditure records, 1842–1906.

Claytons Woollen Mills, Navan: records, 1919–66.

140   Meath Diocesan Archives

Address	The Cathedral
	Mullingar
	County Westmeath
Telephone	(044) 48338
Fax	(044) 40780
E-mail	MULLCATH@iol.ie
Enquiries to	The Archivist

| *Opening hours and facilities* | 10.00–5.00, Mon–Fri, by appointment; photocopying |

Major collections

Documents, exemplaria, correspondence, leases and other material relating to diocesan affairs.

Incomplete series of baptism and marriage records on microfilm and computer, 18th century–.

141 Medical Missionaries of Mary

| *Address* | Beechgrove
Drogheda
County Louth |
Telephone	(041) 983 7512
E-mail	mmmarchives@eircom.net
Enquiries to	The Archivist
Opening hours and facilities	Telephone enquiries, 9.00–5.00; visiting by appointment, 9.00–5.00; photocopying

Major collections

Correspondence and other documents relating to the foundation of the congregation and its administration and works, 1937–.

142 Mercy Congregational Archives

| *Address* | Catherine McAuley Centre
23 Herbert Street
Dublin 2 |
Telephone	(01) 638 7521
Fax	(01) 638 7523
E-mail	mercyarc@indigo.ie
Enquiries to	The Archivist
Opening hours and facilities	By appointment only
photocopying.

Major collections

Mercy International Association Collection of Papers relating to Catherine McAuley and Early Sisters of Mercy, 1778–1870.

Archives of the Sisters of Mercy in the Dublin diocese, 1880–1950 including: rules and constitutions, customs and minor regulations; meditations for retreats; reception and profession ceremonials; prayer books; correspondence; administrative papers, papers relating to convents in the diocese and foundations abroad; and papers relating to the promotion of the Cause of Catherine McAuley.

Archives of Our Lady of Mercy Teacher Training College, Carysfort, Blackrock, County Dublin, 1883–1955 including: administrative papers; architectural plans; reports of the Commissioners of National Education, 1883–1920; reports of the Department of Education, 1924–33; report and programme presented by the national programme conference to the Minister for Education, 1925–1926; programmes of examinations for entrance to the training college and for students in training, 1933–44; college concert programmes; matriculation examination for the National University of Ireland, 1952; correspondence with the Office of National Education, 1900–15; correspondence with the Department of Education, 1922–40; rules and programmes for secondary schools, 1931–49; programmes of primary instruction, 1926–48; rules for national schools, 1934; notes for national teachers issued by the Department of Education, 1933–52; correspondence with the Archbishop of Dublin, 1900–20; golden jubilee celebrations 1952; *Child Education* periodicals 1924; instrumental and vocal scores; articles on Irish educational theory and history; primary school readers.

St Catherine's Convent of Mercy, Baggot Street, Dublin, 1870–1950.

St Brigid's Convent, Naas, County Kildare 1860–1950 including: administrative papers; rules and constitutions; customs and minor regulations; reception and profession ceremonials; hymnals; spiritual reflections.

St John's Convent of Mercy, Birr, County Offaly, 1838–1957 including: specifications for the convent by Edward Welby Pugin, 1838; architectural plans by Pugin & Ashlin, 1855; general specifications and architectural plans, 1909–30; press cuttings; Lenten pastorals of the bishop of Killaloe, 1937–57; letters from bishops of Killaloe, 1866–1939; meditations and considerations for retreats; rules and constitutions; horariums; correspondence, 1847–92; decrees and rulings of the Sacred Congregation for Religious and Secular Institutes, 1926–52; letters regarding the Cause of Catherine McAuley 1937–8; notes on the Crotty schism; history of the convent.

St Michael's Convent of Mercy, Athy, County Kildare, 1852–1954; including: copy letter books of Mother Teresa Maher, 1861–90; novitiate registers, 1855–99; poor account book, 1852–5; receipt account book, 1855–88; summary account book, 1881–92; day account book, 1890–7; minute book of the Children of Mary, 1875–6; architectural plans, 1892–1902; letter from Convent of Mercy, Kinsale, County Cork, regarding the death of a member of their community, 1888; papers relating to a foundation in Brisbane, Australia, 1862–69; administrative papers; rules and constitutions.

Coláiste Ide Preparatory School, Dingle, County Kerry, 1928–55.

St Mary's Convent of Mercy, Arklow, County Wicklow, 1876–1950.

Convent of Mercy, Borrisokane, County Tipperary, 1900–50.

St Michael's Convent of Mercy, Newtownforbes, County Longford, 1869–1950.

The archives also hold the records of some thirty-two industrial schools, residential homes and orphanages run by the Sisters of Mercy. Former residents of the schools and homes may obtain information about their placement by writing to the archives. Access by third parties is restricted under the 100 years' rule. The records include the following:

Antrim	St Patrick's, Crumlin Road, Belfast, 1869–1920
	Whiteabbey, Belfast, 1894–1912
Clare	St Xavier's, Ennis, 1880–1963
	Kilrush, 1870–1956
Cork	Wellington Road, Cork, 1877–86
	St Aloysius, Clonakilty, 1869–1974
	Our Lady of Mercy, Kinsale, 1869–1955
	St Colman's, Rushbrook Cobh, 1870–1987
	St Joseph's, Mallow, 1880–1972
	St Joseph's, Passage West, 1882–1986
Dublin	St Anne's, Booterstown, 1870–1972
	St Vincent's, Goldenbridge, 1880–1985
Galway	St Joseph's, Clifden, 1872–1971
	St Bridget's, Loughrea, 1869–1963
	St Joseph's, Ballinsaloe, 1884–1964
	St Anne's Renmore, Lenaboy, 1869–1966
Kerry	St Joseph's, Killarney, 1869–1986
	Pembroke Alms House/Nazareth, Tralee, 1895–1988
Louth	St Joseph's, Dundalk, 1881–1971
Limerick	St Vincent's, Limerick, 1846–1979
Longford	Our Lady of Succour, Newtownforbes, 1870–1964
Mayo	St Columba's, Westport, 1871–1962
Offaly	St John's, Birr, 1870–1959
Sligo	St Lawrence's, Sligo, 1908–44
Tipperary	Nenagh, 1900–46

	St Augustine's, Templemore, 1870–1964
Tyrone	St Catherine's, Strabane, 1870–1948
Waterfor	St Michael's, Cappoquin, 1873–1987
Westmeath	Mount Carmel, Moate, 1870–1978
	St Joseph's, Summerhill, 1904–64
Wexford	St Michael's, Wexford, 1869–1971
Wicklow	St Kyran's, Rathdrum, 1884–1986

143   Met Éireann (Irish Meteorological Service)

Address	Glasnevin Hill
	Dublin 9
Telephone	(01) 806 4200
Fax	(01) 806 4247
E-mail	met.eireann@met.ie
Website address	www.met.ie
Enquiries to	The Head of Administration or Librarian
Opening hours and facilities	By appointment

Major collections

Manuscript climatological registers from various Irish stations, mid-19th century–.

Administrative files of the Metereological Service, 1936–.

Papers of Dr Leo Wenzel Pollak, former member of the Meteorological Service (b. Prague 1888, d. Dublin 1964).

144   Michael Davitt National Memorial Museum

Address	Land League Place
	Straide
	County Mayo
Telephone	(094) 31022

E-mail	divittmuseum@eircom.net
Website address	www.museumofmayo.com/davitt
Enquiries to	The Museum
Opening hours and facilities	10.00–6.00
Guides	Introductory leaflets

Major collections

Miscellaneous papers relating to Michael Davitt (1846–1906): addresses of welcome, 1882–95; letters and cards, 1898–1905; police reports, 1879–82; photographs, 1879–82; diary of the governor of Dartmoor Prison, 1870–82.

145   Military Archives

Address	Cathal Brugha Barracks Rathmines Dublin 6
Telephone	(01) 804 6457
Fax	(01) 804 6237
Enquiries to	The Military Archivist
Opening hours and facilities	10.00–4.00, by appointment; photocopying

Major collections

The Military Archives is the place of deposit for the records of the Department of Defence, the Defence Forces and the Army Pensions Board.

Collins papers relating to the formation of the IRA, 1919–22.

Liaison papers concerning the period between the Truce and the Civil War, containing correspondence between the Irish and British authorities relating to breaches of the Truce.

The Bureau of Military History, 1913–21: a collection of 1773 witness statements, 334 sets of contemporary documents, 42 photographs, 12 voice recordings, 210 photographs of action sites during Easter Week, press cuttings, assembled between 1947 and 1957 from individuals involved in the activities of the time.

Civil War material including operational and intelligence reports from all commands, July 1922–Mar 1924; copies of radio reports between all commands and the Commander in Chief, Adjutant General, Quarter-master General and Director of Intelligence; Railway Protection Corps, Internment Camps, Press and Publicity and Special Infantry Corps files; orders, instructions and memoranda; documents captured from anti-Treaty forces dealing with operational and intelligence matters; Department of Defence files, 1922–5; complete army census, Nov 1922.

Army Crisis, 1924; Army Organisation Board, 1926; Military Mission to USA, 1926–7; Temporary Plans Division, 1928; Volunteer Force files, 1934–9; internees files; minutes of GHQ Staff Conferences, 1925–39;

Department of Defence files, 1925–47.

Director of Intelligence, Director of Operations, Construction Corps, and Air Defence Command files, 1939–45; GHQ Unit Journals; look out posts log books; minutes of GHQ Conferences and Controller of Censorship files; Air Raid Precautions files.

Director of Operations, 1945–74; Air Corps and Naval Service; United Nations Service, 1958–90; Department of Defence Files, 1947–61.

Copies of handbooks and military publications including *An t-Oglach* and *An Cosantóir.*

*c.*700 private paper collections of retired army personnel.

146   Millmount Museum

Address	Millmount Drogheda County Louth
Telephone	(041) 983 3097
Fax	(041) 984 1599
E-mail	info@millmount.net
Website address	www.millmount.net
Enquiries to	The Supervisor
Opening hours and facilities	10.00–6.00, Mon–Sat; 2.30–6.00, Sun; also by appointment

Major collections

Millmount Museum: catalogue of contents.

Drogheda Union (Board of Guardians): minutes, accounts, register of children, 1858–1923.

River Boyne Company: journal 1790–5.

Drogheda Rowing Club: minute book, 1895–1914.

Drogheda Carpenters and Joiners' Society: minute book, 1867–.
Drogheda Brick and Stone Layers' Society: account book, 1895–1948.

147   Missionary Sisters of the Holy Rosary

Address	Generalate House
	23 Cross Avenue
	Booterstown
	County Dublin
Telephone	(01) 288 1708
Fax	(01) 283 6308
E–mail	mshrgen@eircom.net
Enquiries to	The Archivist
Opening hours and facilities	10.00–5.00, Mon–Fri, by appointment; photocopying

Major collections

Correspondence and documents relating to the foundation of the congregation, 1920–4.

Official documents, reports and correspondence with the Congregation for Religious (Rome), with ecclesiastical authorities and with Mission Houses.

Private correspondence of members of the congregation, including letters of the founder, Bishop Shanahan.

Community annals covering the opening of all missions and their development. General records of the administration and growth of the congregation. Circular letters, bulletins, newsletters and magazines. Biographical material/necrologies.

148   Monaghan County Library

Address	County Library Headquarters
	The Diamond
	Clones
	County Monaghan
Telephone	(047) 51143
Fax	(047) 51863

E-mail	monaghan@eircom.net
Enquiries to	The County Librarian
Opening hours and facilities	By appointment; photocopying

Major collections

Monaghan Grand Jury Presentments, 1811–59.

Records of Carrickmacross, Castleblayney and Clones Poor Law Unions, including minutes and correspondence, 1840–1933; material relating to home assistance and indoor relief, 1909–43.

Monaghan Urban and Rural District Councils minute books, 1899–1968. County Monaghan revised valuation lists, 1902–41.

Crossmaglen Rural District Council minute books and general ledger, 1899–1907.

149 Monaghan County Museum

Address	The Hill Monaghan
Telephone	(047) 82928
Fax	(047) 71189
E-mail	comuseum@monaghancoco.ie
Enquiries to	The Curator
Opening hours and facilities	11.00–1.00, 2.00–5.00, Tue–Fri; Mon by appointment; photocopying

Major collections

Papers from various estates, mostly in County Monaghan but also in County Louth and County Dublin, 18th–20th century.

Marron collection of extracts from records relating to County Monaghan in the Public Record Office, London; State Paper Office, Dublin; marquis of Bath's archives in Longleat House, Wiltshire.

Monaghan County Council: minutes, rate books, ledgers, 1899–1959.

Miscellaneous records of Monaghan Urban District Council, Clones petty sessions, Monaghan County Infirmary, Castleblayney Workhouse, 19th–20th century.

Legal papers relating to the Local Authority (Labourers) Act.

Small collections of papers of Charles Gavan Duffy (1816–1903) and Senator Thomas Toal, 1911–42, and other miscellaneous items.

150   Monaghan Town Council

Address	Town Hall 1 Dublin Street Monaghan
Telephone	(047) 82600
Fax	(047) 84549
E-mail	clerk@monaghantc.ie
Enquiries to	The Town Clerk
Opening hours and facilities	9.15–1.00, 2.00–5.00, Mon–Fri.

Major collections
Records of Monaghan Corporation, 18th–19th century.
Records of Monaghan Urban District Council, 19th–20th century.
Records of Monaghan Town Council, 21st century.

151   Moravian Church in Ireland

Address	25 Church Road Gracehill Ballymena County Antrim
Telephone	(02825) 653141
Enquiries to	The Minister
Opening hours and facilities	By appointment

Major collections
Records (registers of members, baptisms, marriages and burials; minutes; accounts; diaries; deeds) of the Moravian churches in Ballinderry, County Antrim, 1754–1889; Kilwarlin, County Down, 1834–1903; Gracehill, County Antrim, 1719–1987; Dublin, 1748–1980; Cootehill, County Cavan, 1894–1915.
Microfilm copies of these records are available in the Public Record Office of Northern Ireland.

152   Mount Melleray Abbey

Address	Cappoquin County Waterford
Telephone	(058) 54404
Fax	(058) 52140
Enquiries to	The Archivist
Opening hours and facilities	Postal enquiry only
Guides	Pádraig Ó Machain, *Catalogue of Irish manuscripts in Mount Melleray Abbey, County Waterford* (Dublin, DIAS, School of Celtic Studies, 1991).

Major collections
Cistercian antiphoner, 12th century. Cistercian graduale. Latin Vulgate version of the Bible, 13th or 14th century. Collection of Irish manuscripts. Canon W. Burke collection of historical papers.

153   Mount Saint Joseph Abbey

Address	Roscrea County Tipperary
Telephone	(0505) 21711
Fax	(0505) 22198
E-mail	COMMUNITY@MSJROSCREA
Website address	www.iol.ie./~mtjoseph
Enquiries to	The Archivist
Opening hours and facilities	By appointment; letter of reference required; photocopying
Guides	'Lamhscribhinnt Gaeile I Ros Cré', in *Éigse* 37, part II, Geimhreadh 1977–8, p. 216

Major collections
Dr Finbarr Donovan's notes on Irish Cisterian monasteries; Cistercian choir books.

154 Muckross House

Address	Killarney County Kerry
Telephone	(064) 31440
Fax	(064) 33926
E-mail	library@muckross-house.ie
Website address	www.muckross-house.ie
Enquiries to	The Research and Education Officer
Opening hours and facilities	9.00–5.30, Mon–Fri; closed for a week at Christmas; research application forms available for appointments; photocopying

Major collections
Portion of the Kenmare papers relating to the Browne family, formerly earls of Kenmare

155 National Archives

Address	Bishop Street Dublin 8
Telephone	(01) 407 2300
Fax	(01) 407 2333
E-mail	mail@nationalarchives.ie
Website address	www.nationalarchives.ie
Enquiries to	The Director
Opening hours and facilities	10.00–5.00, Mon–Fri; photocopying; photography; microfilming; genealogy advisory service
Guides	*Short guide to the National Archives* (forthcoming); *Short guide to the Public Record Office of Ireland* (1964); *Reports of the Director of the National Archives* (forthcoming); *Reports of the National Archives Advisory*

Council, nos. 1– (1990–). *Reports of the Deputy Keeper of the Public Records in Ireland,* nos. 1–59 (1869–1962) and 60 (forthcoming), nos. 55–60 relate mainly to records accessioned since 1922, nos. 1–54 refer largely to records destroyed in 1922. The records which were destroyed are more fully described in *A guide to the records deposited in the Public Record Office of Ireland,* ed. Herbert Wood (Dublin, 1919). In the case of the National Archives the information contained in *Manuscript sources for the history of Irish civilisation* (Boston, 1965 and 1979) is confined largely to archives accessioned from private sources. Archives deposited in the National Archives through the Business Records Survey of the Irish Manuscripts Commission are reported on in *Irish Economic and Social History* 10– (1985–). Information leaflets, educational facsimiles and off-prints of articles are available for the following topics: Some facts about the National Archives, Sources for genealogy, Sources for local history, Sources for maritime history, Sources for the history of education, Sources for medieval history, Records of the Irish Record Commission, Fenian Documents, Trade Union and labour–related records, Workers in Union, the National School System.

Major collections

Almost all the archives accessioned by the Public Record Office of Ireland before 1922 were destroyed by fire and explosion during the Civil War in June 1922.

Records of Government Departments: The Taoiseach (formerly President of the Executive Council) including records of Dáil Éireann, 1919–22, and Government minutes and associated files, 1922–; Agriculture and Food (originally Agriculture and Technical Instruction), 1899–; Education, including records of the Commissioners of National Education, 1831–1924, the Commissioners of Intermediate Education, 1897–1918, and the modern Department, 1922–; Energy (formerly part of Industry and Commerce), 1920s–; Environment, including orders of the Poor Law Commissioners and the Local Government Board, 1838–1922, and records of the former Department of Local Government and Public Health, 1922–; Finance, 1922–; Foreign Affairs (formerly External Affairs), including records of embassies and consulates in other countries 1919–; Gaeltacht (originally part of the former Department of Lands), 1929–; Health (originally part of the former Department of Local Government and Public

Health), 1920s–; Industry and Commerce, 1922–; Justice (originally Home Affairs), 1922–; Labour (formerly part of Industry and Commerce), 1920s–; The Marine, including records of the former Department of Fisheries and its precursors, 1845–; Social Welfare (formerly parts of Industry and Commerce and the former Department of Local Government and Public Health), 1919–; Tourism, Transport and Communications (formerly parts of Industry and Commerce, the pre-1922 Post Office, and the former Department of Posts and Telegraphs), 1900–. *(Note:* the records of the Department of Defence are held in the Military Archives, q.v.)

Records of other government offices and state agencies including: Chief Secretary's Office, 1790–1924, and its constituent departments, including the Convict Department 1778–1922, the Privy Council Office, 1800–1922, and the Chief Crown Solicitor's Office, mostly 1859–90; Office of the Attorney General, 1922–; Board of Health (Cholera papers), 1832–4; Census of population returns, 1901 and 1911 (complete for all 32 counties) and 1821–51 (fragments for a few counties); Charitable Donations and Bequests, 19th–20th century; Companies Registration Office, 1921–; Office of the Comptroller and Auditor General, 1920s–; Customs and Excise, 1778–1837; Fair Trade Commission, 1953–; Famine Relief Commission, 1845–7; Office of the Governor General, 1922–8; Labour Court, 1946–; National Archives (formerly the Public Record Office of Ireland and the State Paper Office), mostly 1867–; Ordnance Survey, 1824–; Patents Office, 1927–; Office of the Secretary to the President, 1937–; Prison administration records, including the Government Prisons Office, 1836–80, and the General Prisons Board, 1877–1928; Prison registers, 19th–20th century; Proclamations, 17th–19th century; Office of Public Works, 1831–, and its precursors, the Directors General of Inland Navigation, mostly 1800–31, and the Civil Buildings Commissioners, 1802–31; Quit Rent Office, 17th–20th century; Registry of Friendly Societies, *c.*1890–; Royal Hospital Kilmainham, 1684–1829; Shipping agreements and crew lists, 1863–; Tithe Applotment Books, 1828–37; Valuation Office and Boundary Survey, 1827–.

Records of state companies including Aer Lingus, Eircom (Telecom Eireann), Ceimici Teoranta, Dairy Disposal Company, Irish Shipping, Irish Steel, 20th century.

Court and probate records including: Supreme Court, 1924–; Court of Criminal Appeal, 1924; High Court, 1900–13 and 1922–; Probate Office of the High Court (formerly the Principal Probate Registry) and District Probate Registries, mostly 20th century; Circuit Court, Central Criminal Court, County Courts, Grand Juries etc. (transferred by County Registrars, formerly Clerks of the Crown and Peace), mostly late 19th–20th century; Petty Sessions Courts, mostly 1851–1922; Incumbered Estates Court,

Landed Estates Court, Chancery Land Judges, rentals etc., mostly 1850–82; Dáil Éireann Courts, 1920–2; Chancery pleadings, 16th–17th century; a few plea rolls, 14th–15th century.

Registers of baptisms, marriages and burials of the Church of Ireland including: original registers of a few parishes; microfilms of surviving registers of parishes located mainly in dioceses of the south and west of the 26 counties.

Transcripts, calendars, abstracts and indexes of archives which were destroyed in 1922, including: Irish Record Commission (1810–30) calendars of court records, 13th–19th century; Ferguson extracts from Exchequer records, 13th–18th century; Lodge abstracts from Chancery patent rolls, mainly 17th century; Betham, Crosslé, Groves, Grove-White and Thrift collections of genealogical abstracts, mostly 17th–19th century.

In addition to the above, the National Archives holds records accessioned from many other sources, including harbour boards, health boards, hospitals, schools, charities, trade unions, business firms, solicitors' offices, estate offices and private individuals.

156   National Botanic Gardens

Address	Glasnevin Dublin 9
Telephone	(01) 804 0330/804 0332
Fax	(01) 836 0080
E-mail	sball@duchas.ie
Enquiries to	The Librarian
Opening hours and facilities	By appointment; photocopying
Guides	*Occasional Papers. National Botanic Gardens, Glasnevin, Dublin,* Nos. 1, 3 and 4 contain information on archival collections.

Major collections

Official correspondence of the Director, *c.*1870–.

Moore papers: original and photostat copies of family papers and official documents relating to Dr David Moore and Sir Frederick Moore, *c.*1838–1922.

Augustine Henry papers, 1880–1930: annotated books; manuscripts; note-

119

books (including tree books of Henry J. Elwes); Chinese diaries, 1880–99; annotated proofsheets of Elwes & Henry's *Trees of Great Britain and Ireland, 1906–13.*

Botanical correspondence of Natural History Section of National Museum (transferred to National Botanic Gardens in 1970): principal correspondents are N. Colgan, R.L. Praeger, R.A. Phillips and J. Muir.

Watercolours: extensive collection of over 1,500 watercolours of plants cultivated in the Botanic Gardens, 1880–1920, by Lydia Shackleton, Josephine Humphries and Alice Jacob; watercolours by George Victor du Noyer; watercolours of European plants by the Hon. Frederica Plunkett and the Hon. Katherine Plunkett, *c.*1880 (see *Occasional Papers* 3); pen and ink sketches of Irish plants by S. Rosamond Praeger (original drawings for books by her brother, Robert L. Praeger), Burmese plants (mainly orchids), 1900–22, by Lady Charlotte Wheeler-Cuffe.

National College of Art and Design *see* National Irish Visual Arts Library

157   National Gallery of Ireland

Address	Merrion Square Dublin 2
Telephone	(01) 661 5133
Fax	(01) 661 5372
Enquiries to	The Curator of the Centre for Irish Studies & the Yeats Curator
Opening hours and facilities	Postal enquiry only

Major collections

National Gallery archives: Gallery papers from the foundation in the 1860s. Manuscript material on some artists; manuscript material relating to the provenance of paintings in the collection.

Jack B. Yeats archive including miscellaneae, sketchbooks, and the artist's library: *c.* 200 sketchbooks documenting places visited in England, Ireland, New York and Europe, and the characters observed, 1897–1953;

all the artist's published writings, his manuscripts, workbooks, catalogues, presscuttings, postcards, and scrapbooks.

158   National Irish Visual Arts Library

Address	National College of Art & Design 100 Thomas Street Dublin 8
Telephone	(01) 636 4347
Fax	(01) 636 4387
E-mail	romanod@ncad.ie
Website address	www.ncad.ie
Enquiries to	The Administrator
Opening hours and facilities	2.00–8.00, Mon; 9.30–1.00, 2.00–5.00, Tues, Wed, Fri; 9.30–1.00, Thurs; photocopying; photography

Major collections

Over 3000 files of information on 20th century Irish artists: presscuttings, catalogues, ephemera and some manuscript material. Similar files on galleries and related areas: public art, art collections, art and disability, design, craft, fashion.

Irish Exhibition of Living Art, 1947–71: documentary material from the collection of the late Anne Yeats.

Library of Evie Hone (1894–1955) including some manuscript material and sketches.

Egan collection: scrapbooks relating to the running of a Dublin gallery in the 1920s.

Earley Company: records of manufacturers of church furnishings.

Records of the Cultural Relations Committee, 1949–52.

Kilkenny Design Centre: documentary material including newspaper clippings and slides.

Archives of the National College of Art and Design: records of all enrolled students, 1877–1940s; reports and other material relating to the administration of the College, 20th century.

Friends of the National Collections: complete archive, on loan for ten years, searchable on in-house database.

159   National Library of Ireland

Address	Kildare Street Dublin 2
Telephone	(01) 603 0200
Fax	(01) 676 6690
E-mail	info@nli.ie
Website address	www.nli.ie
Enquiries to	The Keeper of Manuscripts
Opening hours and facilities	10.00–8.30, Mon–Wed; 10.00–4.30, Thurs–Fri; 10.00–12.30, Sat; Manuscripts are not issued 12.30–2.00 and 5.00–6.00, or after 7.00. Readers' tickets, for which identification is required, are issued in the main Library building; photography
Guides	R.J. Hayes (ed.), *Manuscript sources for the history of Irish civilisation* (Boston, 1965), and *Supplement* (Boston, 1978); *Catalogue of Irish manuscripts in the National Library of Ireland* (Dublin, 1967–); Noel Kissane (ed.), *Treasures of the National Library of Ireland* (Drogheda, 1994); major accessions noted in annual *Report of the Council of Trustees of the National Library of Ireland.* For material catalogued since 1990, see the on-liner catalogue at www.nli.ie

Major collections

The collection amounts to 65,000 catalogued manuscripts comprising 750,000 individual items. There is also a special collection of 28,000 deeds. In addition there are a number of collections of estate papers which have not yet been fully processed. The collection is composed almost entirely of material of Irish interest. It is extremely diverse and the following outline is no substitute for a careful study of the catalogues.

Estate papers constitute the main component of the collection. Among the more notable estates represented are Balfour (Counties Louth and Meath), Bellew (County Galway), Castletown (County Laois), Clements (Counties Leitrim and Donegal), Clonbrock (County Galway), Conyngham (Counties Meath, Donegal, Clare and Limerick), Coolatin (County Wicklow), de Freyne (County Roscommon), de Vesci (County Laois),

Doneraile (County Cork), Farnham (County Cavan), Fingal (County Dublin), ffrench (County Galway), Gormanston (County Meath), Headford (County Meath), Inichiquin (County Clare), Lismore (County Waterford), Louth (Counties Meath, Louth, Monaghan and Kildare), Mahon (County Galway), Mansfield (County Kildare), Monteagle (County Limerick), O'Hara (County Sligo), Ormond (Counties Kilkenny and Tipperary), Powerscourt (County Wicklow), Prior-Wandesforde (County Kilkenny), Sarsfield (County Cork), Westport (County Mayo), Wicklow (County Wicklow), Wynne (County Wicklow). Most of the collections date from the 17th to the 20th century but the Ormond papers include a collection of deeds extending back to the arrival of the Normans in the 12th century.

The collection represents most of the nationalist movements from the 18th century onwards, and includes papers of Wolfe Tone, Daniel O'Connell and James Fintan Lalor. The Land War and Home Rule periods are represented by the papers of T.C. Harrington, T.P. Gill, William O'Brien, J.F.X. O'Brien and John Redmond. The period 1916–23 is particularly well documented and the collection includes papers of Sir Roger Casement, Erskine Childers, Thomas McDonagh, Bulmer Hobson, Eoin MacNeill, Dean T. O'Kelly and Patrick Pearse. The labour and trade union movements are represented by the papers of Thomas Johnson and William O'Brien.

The collection includes a number of substantial business archives including those of the Prior-Wandesforde Collieries, Castlecomer, Avoca Mines and Locke's Distillery, Kilbeggan.

The Kilmainham Papers consist of 377 volumes of records of the commanders-in-chief of the forces in Ireland, and provide detailed information on recruitment, personnel, supplies, encampments and movements of troops for the period 1780–1890.

Among the writers who are represented are Richard Brinsley Sheridan, Maria Edgeworth, Canon Sheehan, George Moore, John Millington Synge, George Bernard Shaw, Sean O'Casey, Patrick Kavanagh, Brendan Behan, Benedict Kiely, James Plunkett, Hugh Leonard, Brien Friel and Tom McIntyre. Of particular importance are the large collection of papers of W.B. Yeats and James Joyce.

The collection of Gaelic manuscripts amounts to 1236 volumes or folders, dating from the 14th century onwards. The most notable accession was a collection of 178 volumes purchased at the Phillipps sale in 1931. Subject area represented are genealogy, hagiography, religion, medicine, law and *dinnseanchas* (place-lore). The bardic tradition is represented by the earliest surviving example of a book of praise poetry, the 14th-century *duanaire* of Tomas Mag Shamhradhain of Tullyhaw,

County Cavan, known as the Book of Magauran. Among the later writers whose work is represented are Aodhagán Ó Rathaille, Peader Ó Doirnin, Eoghan Ruadh Ó Súilleabháin, Brian Merriman and Tomas Ó Criomhtháin.

There is an extensive collection of maps and plans of Irish interest over half of which are estate maps which were acquired with estate collections. They are supplemented by 4,000 file copies of estate maps produced by the Dublin firm of surveyors, Brownrigg, Longfield and Murray in the period 1775–1833, which include material for most counties. Notable items in the map collection include a map of Europe in a 12th-century copy of the *Topographia Hiberniae* of Giraldus Cambrensis, maps by Francis Jobson and Richard Bartlett documenting the Tudor conquest, and plans of fortifications in the period 1685–92 by Captain Thomas Phillips and the Huguenot engineer John Goubet. Also of interest are a set of 18th-century copies of William Petty's Down Survey, a set of over 200 coloured maps of mail coach roads, 1805–16, and a set of maps of the bogs of Ireland, 1810–13.

The National Library also has an extensive collection of microfilm copies of material of Irish interest in archives and libraries overseas, much of it relating to the early medieval period.

160   National Museum of Ireland

Address	Collins Barracks
	Benburb Street
	Dublin 7
Telephone	(01) 677 7444
Fax	(01) 677 7498
E-mail	sfrawley@museum.ie
Enquiries to	The Registrar
Opening hours and facilities	10.00–5.00, Tue–Fri; by appointment; photocopying; photography

Major collections

Correspondence relating to the administration of the Museum and the acquisition of items now in the collections.

Archives of the Natural History Museum including notebooks and journals of naturalists whose collections are held by the Museum, 1850–.

161   National Photographic Archive

Address	Meeting House Square
	Temple Bar
	Dublin 2
Telephone	(01) 603 0200
Fax	(01) 677 7451
E-mail	photoarchive@nli.ie
Website	www.nli.ie
Enquiries to	The Curator
Opening hours and facilities	10.00–5.00, Mon–Fri; access to the Reading Room by reader's ticket; reprographic services include the provision of photographic prints, transparencies and slides
Guides	Sarah Rouse, *Into the light: an illustrated guide to the photographic collections of the National Library of Ireland* (Dublin, 1998); general information leaflets

Major collections

Collections of portrait and postcard studios include the Lawrence collection (40,000 glass negatives of topographical scenes, 1870–1914), Stereo Pairs collection (3,059 glass negatives, mainly picturesque views, 1860–83), Eblana collection (3,000 glass negatives of topographical scenes, 1870–90), Eason collection (4,000 glass negatives for Eason postcard series, 1900–40), Valentine collection (3,000 glass negatives for the Valentine postcard series, 1900–60), Poole collection (60,000 glass negatives from the studio of A.H. Poole, Waterford, 1884–1954), Keogh collection (330 glass negatives of Dublin, 1915–30, from the Keogh Brothers studio), Morgan collection (aeriel views of Ireland, mid–1950s), Cardall collection (5,000 negatives for Cardall postcard series, 1950s–60s), Wiltshire collection (1,330 images taken by Elinor Wiltshire, mainly of Dublin, 1951–70s).

Other important photographic collections include the Clonbrock collection (2,000 glass plates taken by the Dillon Family, Barons Clonbrock, 1860–1930), O'Dea collection (railways in Ireland, 1937–66), Wynne collection (County Mayo, 1867–1960).

Smaller collections include good coverage of events during 1916, the War of Independence and the Civil War, as well as other political and social events.

Over 300 photographic albums covering a wide range of subjects.

162 National Theatre Archive

Address	The Abbey Theatre 26 Lower Abbey Street Dublin 1
Telephone	(01) 887 2200
Fax	(01) 872 9177
E-mail	archive@abbeytheatre.ie
Website address	www.abbeytheatre.ie; www.abbeytheatrearchives.ie (from 1 November 2004)
Enquiries to	The Archivist
Opening hours and facilities	By appointment only

Major collections

Archives of the National Theatre Society Limited and related material on the history and development of theatre in Ireland, which provides a context for the history and development of the Abbey Theatre, dating from its foundation in 1904. The collection includes handbills, posters, scripts, prompt scripts, programmes, presscuttings, music scores; early stage management records; stage plans and drawings, production photographs, model boxes; a large collection of administrative records including logbooks of plays received, financial records and correspondence.

163 National University of Ireland

Address	49 Merrion Square Dublin 2
Telephone	(01) 676 7246/676 3429
Fax	(01) 661 9665
E-mail	registrar@nui.ie
Website address	www.nui.ie
Enquiries to	The Registrar

Opening hours   9.15–1.00, 2.15–5.00, Mon–Fri; by appointment;
and facilities

Major collections
Royal University of Ireland: minutes of the Senate, 1880–1908, of the Standing Committee, 1883–1909, and of the Medical, Library and other occasional committees, 1891–1908; financial records, 1881–1908; copy letter books, 1880–1908; matriculation application forms and printed matter including calendars and examination papers, 1883–1909.
National University of Ireland: minutes of the Senate, Standing Committee, Finance Committee, and General Board of Studies with supporting documents, 1908–; correspondence, 1909–; statutes, 1911–; printed matter including calendars, examination results, sessional and honours lists, 1911–.

164   National University of Ireland, Cork Boole Library

Address   University College
                   Cork

Telephone   (021) 490 3180

Fax   (021) 427 3428

E-mail   c.quinn@ucc.ie

Website address booleweb.ucc.ie/search/subject/archives/archives.htm

Enquiries to   The Archivist

Opening hours   9.30–1.00, 2.30–4.45, Mon–Fri; early closing 4.15,
and facilities   June–Sept; appointment necessary;
                   photocopying; photography

Major collections
Estate papers: Ryan of Inch, *c.*1700–1953; Grehan, 1709–1970; Bantry House collection, *c.*1694–1980.
Political papers: Attic Press/Roisin Conry collection, *c.*1970–97; Neville Keery papers, 1959–87; Thomas McDonagh/Padraig MacSuibhne correspondence, 1903–15.
Literary papers: John V. Kelleher correspondence, 1948–83; Peter Davison collection, 1965–83; Nancy McCarthy collection, 20th century.
Peters photographic collection, World War II.

165 National University of Ireland, Cork College Archives

Address	Heritage and Visual Arts Office
	West Lodge
	University College
	Cork
Telephone	(021) 490 3552/490 2753
Fax	(021) 903555
E-mail	v.teehan@ucc.ie
Website	www.ucc.ie
Enquiries to	The University Archivist
Opening hours and facilities	10.00–5.00, Mon–Fri; by appointment;

Major collections

Archives of University College, Cork, 1845–c.1960, reflecting the educational, administrative and social aspects of the College since its foundation as Queen's College Cork, including identifiable series originating from College offices such as the Office of the President, Vice-President, Registrar, Finance Officer and Secretary, College Engineer, and Librarian.

Admission records; recent examination results, 1930–.

Records relating to individual academic departments, c.1925–.

Computerised data base of title deeds of College buildings and lands, cross-referenced to the series of architectural maps and plans of the College.

Minute books of College committees, and of student clubs and societies.

College publications including staff newsletters, student magazines and pamphlets produced by the College. Reference collection of published work relevant to the College, its history, to individuals associated with the College, and the College's role in the community.

Collection of photographs documenting the evolution of the College, mid-19th century–.

Private paper collections of individuals associated with UCC including Professor Aloys Fleischmann and Professor James Hogan.

UCC oral history collection.

166

National University of Ireland, Cork
Special Collections and Archives

Address	Boole Library University College Cork
Telephone	(021) 490 2282
Fax	(021) 427 3428
E-mail	specialcollections@ucc.ie
Website address	booleweb.ucc.ie/search/subject/speccol/speccol.htm
Opening hours and facilities	9.00–8.15, Mon–Fri (term); 9.30–4.45, Mon–Fri and (vacation), 9.30–4.14, Mon–Fri, July–Sept; advance notice and identification required; photocopying and microfilm printouts
Guides	Padraig de Brun, *Clár Lámhscríbhinní Gaeilge Choláiste Ollscoile Chorcai: Cnusach Thórna*; Brendan Ó Conchuir, *Clár Lámhscríbhinní Gaelige Choláiste Ollscoile Chorcai: Cnuasach Uí Mhurchú* (Dublin, 1991)

Major collections

Gaelic manuscripts: Torna Collection containing manuscripts which belonged to Professor Tadg Ó Donnchadha, professor of Irish in UCC (1916–44); manuscripts of professor J.E.H. Murphy, professor of Irish in Trinity College, Dublin (1896–1919); manuscripts of Canon Power, lecturer and later professor of Archaeology in UCC (1915–32).

Non-Gaelic manuscripts: papers of eminent professors such as George Boole, Tadg Ó Donnchadha, Daniel Corkery, Cormac Ó Cuilleanáin; papers of William O'Brien; Kinsale manorial records; several manuscript estate maps, music scores, minor Middle Eastern and Far Eastern manuscripts.

National University of Ireland, Dublin *see*
University College Dublin

167 National University of Ireland, Galway James Hardiman Library

Address	National University of Ireland Galway
Telephone	(091) 524411 ext. 3636
Fax	(091) 522394
E-mail	kieran@sulacco.library.ucg.ie
Website address	www.library.nuigalway.ie
Enquiries to	The Archivist
Opening hours and facilities	9.30–1.15, 2.30–5.00, Mon–Fri; appointment advisable; photocopying; photography by arrangement
Guides	Published work on the Corporation MSS can be found in Royal Commission on Historical Manuscripts, *10th Report* (1885), 380–520 and in various issues of the *Galway Archaeological & Historical Society Journal*. See M. Hayes-McCoy 'The Eyre Documents in University College Galway' in *GAHSJ* 20 (1942).

Major collections

Minute books of Galway Corporation, Galway Town Commissioners, 15th–19th century; minute books of Galway Urban Sanitary Authority, late 19th century.

The Hyde MSS Collection, bequeathed by Douglas Hyde, containing volumes of prose, poetry and various tracts penned by scribes, 18th century–, and including miscellaneous manuscripts of Douglas Hyde.

Manuscripts in the Irish language and items reflecting the Gaelic revival are included in collections such as the papers of Stiophán Bairéad and Tadgh Seoige.

Richie-Pickow collection of over 5,000 photographs and some traditional music material gathered by an American couple in Ireland, 1952–3.

Collections relating to academics and organizations within the College including papers of *An Stoc* newspaper, 1924–8; out-letter book of Professor J.E. Cairnes, 1865–7; papers of Richard O'Doherty, professor of midwifery, 1849–76; papers of Mary O'Donovan, professor of history, 1914–57.

Landed estates collections including the Wilson Lynch family, Belvoir, County Clare, *c.*1860–1930; Eyre family, 1720–1857; O'Connor Donelan family, Sylane, Tuam, 1794–1930; O'Callighan collection (including papers relating to the Bodyke evictions); Castle Taylor, Ardrahan, County Galway; Daly family, Dunsandle, Loughrea; some material of the ffrench family of Ballyglunin.

Business collections including legal papers relating to the Clifden–Galway railway.

Political collections including those of James Fitzgerald-Kenney, Dr Byran Cusack and Frank J. Carty.

Theatre collections including those of the Druid Theatre and *An Taibhdearc*.

Private papers including papers relating to the will of Annie Barnacle; Stock letters, 1808–32; and many small collections.

168 National University of Ireland, Maynooth Russell Library

Address	Maynooth County Kildare
Telephone	(01) 708 3890
Fax	(01) 628 6008
E-mail	Penny.Woods@may.ie
Website address	www.may.ie/library
Enquiries to	The Librarian, Russell Library
Opening hours and facilities	10.00–1.00, 2.00–5.00, Mon–Thurs; appointment advisable; photography
Guides	Paul Walsh, *Catalogue of Irish manuscripts in Maynooth College Library* (Ma Nuad, 1943); Pádraig Ó Fiannachta, *Clár lámhscríbhinní Gaeilge Ma Nuad,* fasc. 2–8 (Ma Nuad, 1965–73); Pádraig Ó Fiannachta, *Leabharlanna na cleire II* (Institiúid Ard–Leinn Bhaile Átha Cliath, 1980); Pádraig de Brún, *Lámhscríbhinní Gaeilge: treoir-liosta* (Institiúid Ard-Leinn Bhaile Átha Cliath, 1988); R.W. Richardson (ed.), *The Salamanca letters: a cata-logue of correspondence, 1691–1871* (Maynooth, 1995); Agnes Neligan (ed.), *Maynooth Library treasures* (Dublin, 1995).

Major collections

120 volumes of Irish manuscripts copied for or collected, *c.*1820, by Dr John Murphy, bishop of Cork (1771–1847); includes romances, religious and secular poetry, sermons, translations of devotional works, lives of saints and genealogies.

*c.*100 Irish manuscripts collected by Eugene O'Curry (1796–1862), and additional material transcribed by him. 30 volumes of Irish manuscripts collected by Dr Laurence Renehan, president of the College (1845–57).

Illuminated manuscripts and books of hours; other medieval manuscripts in Latin including liturgical works, commentaries on scripture and canon law, and 18th century student notebooks from Irish continental colleges.

Manuscript material in English including Laurence Renehan's historical papers and transcripts, antiquarian papers of Revd John Shearman, Canon O'Hanlon's notes for his *Lives of the Saints,* and literary items such as 'The Master', a play by Patrick Pearse.

National University of Ireland, Maynooth *see also* St Patrick's College, Maynooth

169   New Ross Port Company

Address	Harbour Office New Ross County Wexford
Telephone	(051) 421303
Fax	(051) 421294
E-mail	ceo@newrossport.iol.ie
Enquiries to	The Chief Executive
Opening hours and facilities	By appointment; photocopying

Major collections

Minute books, 1848–1986; shipping books, 1958–; letterbooks and correspondence, 1927–40, 1980–; register of vessels, 1848–91; register of mortgages, 1851–76; ledgers, 1848–1900 and other financial records.

170 Newbridge House

Address	Donabate County Dublin
Telephone	(01) 843 6534
Fax	(01) 843 6535
Enquiries to	The Curator
Opening hours and facilities	By appointment
Guides	Information leaflets available

Major collections

Newbridge House account books, 18th century; farm diary, 1840–2; land survey map, 1747.

Pilkington family papers including material relating to the life of John Pilkington; correspondence and memoirs of Laetitia Pilkington; and poems of the Revd Matthew Pilkington corrected by Dean Swift, 18th century.

Cobbe family papers including the diary of Colonel Alexander Cobbe VC, 1894, and the journal of Archbishop Charles Cobbe, 1742–3.

171 Newry and Mourne Museum

Address	Arts Centre 1a Bank Parade Newry County Down BT35 6HP
Telephone	(02830) 266232
Fax	(02830) 266839
E-mail	museum@newryandmourne.gov.uk
Website address	www.newryandmourne.gov.uk
Enquiries to	The Curator
Opening hours and facilities	10.30–1.00, 2.00–4.30, Mon–Fri; photocopying

Major collections

The Reside collection: estate records (rentals, deeds, maps and surveys) of the earls of Kilmorey, marquises of Downshire, Hall family of Narrow Water and other local landowning families; maps, Encumbered Estates records, Land Purchase Commission papers, legal papers, architectural plans and note books, miscellaneous items relating to south Armagh, south Down and north Louth, 18th–late 20th century.

Registers of protests for Newry port, 1902–69.

Correspondence and records of Joseph Fisher & Son Ltd, early 20th century.

Syllabuses, programnmes and posters for Newry Musical Feis, 1932–3 & 1953–98 and for Newry Drama Festival, 1949–.

Miscellaneous ephemera and manuscripts relating to individuals, local businesses and organizations, local events and various aspects of local history, 18th–20th century.

Photographic and slide collection, 19th–20th century.

172   North Down Heritage Centre

Address	Town Hall
	Bangor Castle
	Bangor
	County Down
Telephone	(02891) 271200
Fax	(02891) 271370
E-mail	heritage@northdown.gov.uk
Website address	www.northdown.gov.uk/heritage
Enquiries to	The Manager
Opening hours and facilities	10.20–4.30, Tue–Sat; 2.00–4.30, Sun; photocopying; photography

Major collections

Miscellaneous local authority records relating especially to the harbour, gas supply and public health, early 20th century–.

Volume of 64 maps of the North Down and Strangford Lough areas by Thomas Raven, 17th century.

Memorabilia relating to Percy French.

173 North-Eastern Education and Library Board

Address   Local Studies Service
                   Demense Avenue
                   Ballymena
                   County Antrim BT43 7BG

Telephone   (02825) 664121

E-mail   yvonne.hirst@neelb.org.uk

Website address www.neelb.org.uk

Opening hours   10.00–8.00, Mon, Thurs, Fri, 10.00–5.30, Tue, Wed,
and facilities   10.00–5.00, Sat; photocopying, microfilm printouts

Major collections
Records from over 80 public elementary schools in counties Antrim and
   Londonderry: mostly post-1945 roll books but also some earlier roll books
   and daily report books.

174 Offaly County Library

Address   O'Connor Square
                   Tullamore

Telephone   (0506) 46834

Fax   (0506) 52769

E-mail   libraryhq@offalycoco.ie

Website address www.offaly.ie

Enquiries to   The Local Studies Librarian/Archivist

Opening hours   By appointment
and facilities

Major collections
Local authority archives including those of the Grand Juries, Boards of
   Guardians, County, Urban and Rural District Councils, Town Commis-
   sioners, Boards of Health and Assistance, Committee of Agriculture, Joint
   Burial Boards, Drainage Boards.

Business records and private papers including the Ridley collection, Charleville and Howard Bury papers, Goodbody collection, Perry collection, Hoey and Denning solicitors' collection.
Map collections and local folk song collection.

175   Cardinal Tomás Ó Fiaich Memorial Library

Address	15 Moy Road Armagh Co. Armagh BT61 7LY
Telephone	(02837) 522981
Fax	(02837) 511944
E-mail	eolas@ofiaich.ie
Website address	www.ofiaich.ie
Enquiries to	The Librarian
Opening hours and facilities	9.30–1.00, 2.00–5.00, Mon–Fri; letter of introduction and appointment necessary; photocopying, photography, digital imaging
Guides	Raymond Murray 'The Armagh diocesan archives', in *Archivium Hibernicum* 32 (1974), 93–7

Major collections
Archives of the archdiocese of Armagh, including correspondence of archbishops and documents relating to parishes and clergy, 1787–1953.
Overseas archive (in partnership with University College, Dublin): transcripts and translations of 250,000 documents relating to the Irish experience overseas, especially in France and Spain, 16th–19th century.

176   Omagh Library

Address	Spillars Place Omagh County Tyrone BT78 1HL
Telephone	(02882) 244821

Fax	(02882) 246716
E-mail	Omagh-library@welbni.org
Website address	www.welbni.org
Enquiries to	The Senior Librarian
Opening hours and facilities	9.15–4.30, Mon, Wed, Fri, 9.15–8.00, Tue, Thurs, 9.15–8.00, 9.15–1.00, 2.00–5.00, Sat; photocopying and microfilm printouts

Major collections

National school records from West Tyrone including Calkill, Beltany, Deverney, Edenderry, Carnkenny, Erganagh and Tattykeeran, 20th century.

Duplicate valuation records for the Rural Dictrict Council areas of Omagh, Castlederg, Clogher and Strabane, 1920–57.

177 Oireachtas Library

Address	Leinster House Kildare Street Dublin 2
Telephone	(01) 618 3412
Fax	(01) 618 4376
E-mail	lib@oireachtas.ie
Wesbsite address	www.oireachtas.ie
Enquiries to	The Librarian
Opening hours and facilities	Admission to the Library is normally restricted to members of the Oireachtas and Oireachtas officials. Members of the public will only be admitted by permission of the Ceann Comhairle [Speaker]. Access should then be arranged with the Librarian; photocopying

Major collections

Manuscript records of trials conducted by the Special Commission (Fenianism), 1866.

Miscellaneous reports on aspects of Irish affairs including ports, gaols, public records and the work of public offices, 17th–19th century.

178   Ordnance Survey of Northern Ireland

Address	Colby House Stranmillis Court Malone Lower Belfast BT9 5BJ
Telephone	(02890) 255755
Fax	(02890) 255700
E-mail	osni@nics.gov.uk
Website address	www.osni.gov.uk
Enquiries to	The Director
Opening hours and facilities	9.15–4.30, Mon–Fri;

Major collections
Major collection of maps and aerial films of Northern Ireland: 6" county series maps, 1830–1900; 6" and 25" county series maps, 1900–50; Irish grid series maps at all scales and aerial films, 1950–.

179   Ossory Diocesan Archives

Address	Sion House Kilkenny
Telephone	(056) 62448
Fax	(056) 63753
E-mail	bishop@ossory.ie
Website address	www.ossory.ie
Enquiries to	The Bishop of Ossory
Opening hours and facilities	By appointment; photocopying

Major collections
Papers and correspondence of bishops and priests, 1639–.

180   Passionist Fathers

Address   St Paul's Retreat
                   Mount Argus
                   Kimmage Road
                   Dublin 6W

Telephone   (01) 499 2000

Fax   (01) 499 2001

E-mail   archivesmtargus@eircom.net

Enquiries to   The Archivist

Opening hours   By appointment; photocopying
and facilities

Major collections
Archives of Mount Argus but including material relating to other Passionist
   houses in Ireland, Scotland and Botswana.
Records of Passionist personnel, 1805–; diary recording the early days of
   Mount Argus in 7 vols; chronicles; accounts; *Cross,* monthly magazine,
   1910–80.
Journal by Fr Pius Devine of his journey through the Americas, 1880s, on
   a lecturing tour to reduce the debt of Mount Argus.

181   Patrician Brothers
         (Brothers of St Patrick)

Address   Kingston House
                   Kingston
                   Galway

Telephone   (091) 523267

Enquiries to   The Archivist

Opening hours   Postal enquiry; photocopying
and facilities

Major collections
Material relating to the origins of the Patrician Brothers and to houses in

Ireland, 1808–1960; in India, 1875–1960; in Australia, 1883–1960; in Papua New Guinea, 1960–; and in California, 1947–60.

Correspondence of the Superior General, 1880–1960.

Diaries and travel accounts of some members of the congregation.

Correspondence, mainly personal, notebooks and account books, 1829–1960.

Printed matter including chapter studies and constitutions, 1880–1986.

182   Pearse Museum

Address	St Enda's Park
	Rathfarnham
	Dublin 14
Telephone	(01) 493 4208
Fax	(01) 493 6120
Enquiries to	The Curator
Opening hours and facilities	10.00–1.00 daily; 2.00–5.30, Oct–Mar; 2.00–6.00, Apr–Sep

Major collections

Documents, photographs and personal effects relating to Patrick Pearse (1879–1916) and the history of St Enda's.

183   Presbyterian Historical Society

Address	Church House
	Fisherwick Place
	Belfast BT1 6DW
Telephone	(02890) 322284
Enquiries to	The Assistant Secretary
Opening hours and facilities	10.00–12.30, Mon–Fri; 1.15–3.30, Wed; photocopying
Guides	Annual *Bulletin of the Presbyterian Historical Society of Ireland*

Major collections
Records of the General Synod of Ulster and the Seceders and, since 1840, of the General Assembly of the Presbyterian Church in Ireland.
Records relating to some presbyteries and congregations; baptismal and marriage records of many congregations; files detailing records held by congregations.
Files on ministers of the Presbyterian Church in Ireland from 1613.
Writings by Presbyterian ministers.
Copies, by Tenison Groves, of census records.
Communion tokens and artefacts relating to Presbyterianism.

184   Presentation Sisters

Address	Presentation Mission House Lucan County Dublin
Telephone	(01) 628 0540/ 628 0305/628 2467
Fax	(01) 628 2467
Enquiries to	The Archivist
Opening hours and facilities	10.00–12.00, 2.00–5.30, Mon–Fri; by appointment; photocopying

Major collections
Material relating to Nano Nagle (18th century) and to the work of Presentation Sisters in Ireland, England, Africa, India and Pakistan, USA.

185   Public Record Office of Northern Ireland

Address	66 Balmoral Avenue Belfast BT9 6NY
Telephone	(02890) 255905
Fax	(02890) 255999
E-mail	proni@dcalni.gov.uk

Website address	www.proni.gov.uk
Enquiries to	The Head of Public Services
Opening hours and facilities	9.00–4.45, Mon–Wed & Fri, 10.00–8.45, Thurs; annual closure for weeks in Nov/Dec; photocopying; microfilming
Guides	*Reports of the Deputy Keeper of the Records, 1923–87; Annual Report, 1991–5; Statutory Reports, 1995–.* Sectional lists on textile industry records, landed estate, tithes, church registers, maps and plans, electoral registers, and educational records. Recent publications include *Guide to sources for women's history, Guide to county sources – Fermanagh, Armagh, Tyrone, Monaghan.* A full list of publications is available on request.

Major collections

Records of the principal departments of government from the 1920s: papers of the Northern Ireland Cabinet, 1922–.

Records of the Crown and County Courts, 18th century–; records of Borough, County, Urban and Rural District councils, 19th century–, and in some cases, 18th century–.

Ordnance Survey maps, 1830–1970; tithe applotment books, 1823–38; valuation records comprising maps and valuation lists, 1828–; records of the Boards of Guardians, 1838–1948; records of some 2,500 national schools, 1832–70.

Private records: landed estate records including title deeds, agents' reports, correspondence, rentals, household accounts, estate maps, valuations and surveys; large collection of business records including the records of over 250 linen companies; a wide range of solicitors' records, emigrant letters, and the papers of private societies and organisations, copies of church records, including parish registers.

186   Queen's University of Belfast

Address	Main Library Queen's University Belfast BT7 1NN
Telephone	(02890) 273607
Fax	(02890) 323340

Major collections

Archives of the University, 1909–, and of its predecessors, Queen's College, 1845–1909, Queen's University in Ireland, 1850–82, and the Royal University of Ireland, 1881–1909.

Scientific papers and correspondence of Thomas Andrews, 1828–76, and James Thomson, 1857–92.

Musical manuscripts collected and compiled by Edward Bunting, 1792–1943. Original works by Sir Hamilton Harty, 1900–39.

Literary manuscripts of Arthur O'Shaughnessy, *c.*1863–70; Edith Somerville and Violet Martin, 1873–1948; Helen Waddell, 1909–50; Shan Bullock, 1889–1935.

Correspondence and classical and other papers of R.M. Henry, 1899–1941. Personal papers of Sir Robert Hart, inspector general of the Chinese Imperial Maritime Customs, 1854–1908, and of Stanley F. Wright, commissioner of the Chinese Imperial Maritime Customs, 1850–1951.

187 Raphoe Diocesan Archives/ Cartlann Ratha-Bhoth

Telephone	(074) 21208
Enquiries to	The Bishop's House
E-mail	raphoe@indigo.ie
Websute address	www.raphoediocese.com
Opening hours and facilities	Postal enquiry only; photocopying

Major collections

The archives, only recently established, is in the process of formation. It is essentially the episcopal archives, beginning with Bishop James McDevitt (1870–9). Papers of Bishops Daniel McGettigan, Michael Logue and Patrick O'Donnell are being acquired from Armagh Diocesan Archives (q.v.).

188 Redemptorist Fathers (Congregation of the Most Holy Redeemer)

Address	Liguori House 75 Orwell Road Dublin 6
Telephone	(01) 492 2688
Enquiries to	The Archivist
Opening hours and facilities	By appointment; photocopying

Major collections

Material relating to the history of Irish Redemptorists in Ireland, Australia, the Philippines, Brazil and India; to personnel; to the foundation and development of various Irish houses.

Material relating to apostolic works in Ireland including missions, the holy family confraternity and the Perpetual Novena to Our Lady of Perpetual Help.

Collections of sermons and of retreats to priests and religious; material relating to Irish retreat houses and new apostolates at home and abroad; house annals, 1851–.

189   Registry of Deeds

Address   Henrietta Street
Dublin 1

Telephone   (01) 670 7500; LoCall 1890 333001

Fax   (01) 804 8406

E-mail   susan.cullen@landreg.ie

Website address www.irlgov.ie/landreg/

Enquiries to   The Senior Assistant Registrar

Opening hours 10.00–4.30, Mon–Fri; photocopying
and facilities

Guides   Margaret Dickson Falley, *Irish and Scotch-Irish ancestral research* (2 vols) P.B. Eustace (ed.), *Registry of Deeds, abstract of wills* vol. i, *1708–45* (1956); do., vol. ii, *1746–85* (1954); Eilish Ellis & P.B. Eustace (eds), vol. iii, *1785–1832* (Dublin, 1984); Peter Roebuck, 'The Irish Registry of Deeds', *Irish Historical Studies* 18, no. 69 (Mar 1972); P.B. Phair, 'Guide to the Registry of Deeds', *Analecta Hibernica* 23 (1966)

Major collections
Records of registered deeds of transfer of ownership or interest in property, 1708–, records of wills, 1708–1832. Some records of marriage settlements.
This office maintains an index of names of grantors, 1708–, and an index of placenames, 1708–1947, to all our records.

190   Religious Society of Friends Historical Library

Address   Swanbrook House
Bloomfield Avenue
Morehampton Road
Donnybrook
Dublin 4

Telephone	(01) 668 7157
Enquiries to	The Curator
Opening hours and facilities	11.00–1.00, Thur; photocopying
Guides	O.C. Goodbody *Guide to Irish Quaker records, 1654–1860* (1967); P.B. Eustace & O.C. Goodbody *Abstracts of wills and inventories, 17th & 18th century* (1957)

Major collections

Quaker records, minute books, family lists, sufferings, testimonies of denial, disownments, 17th–20th century.

Letters and documents relating to relief work in the Great Famine.

Registers of births, marriages and burials, 17th–20th century.

Collections of letters, 18th–20th century.

Diaries; records of Quaker schools in Ireland; collection of photograph albums and scrapbooks.

Museum items: samplers, embroidery, dress.

Pedigrees, wills, deeds, marriage certificates, 17th–20th century.

Pamphlets and correspondence related to Quaker mission and service.

191   Religious Society of Friends Ulster Quarterly Meeting

Address	Friends Meeting House 4 Magheralave Road Lisburn BT28 3BD County Antrim
Enquiries to	The Archives Committee
Opening hours and facilities	Postal enquiry only
Guides	O.C. Goodbody, *Guide to Irish Quaker records, 1654–1860* (Dublin, 1967)

Major collections

Records of the Society of Friends in Ulster from 1673: minutes of meetings; births, marriages and death records; sufferings. These records are also available on microfilm in the Public Record Office of Northern Ireland (q.v.).

192   Representative Church Body Library

Address	Braemor Park
	Churchtown
	Dublin 14
Telephone	(01) 492 3979
Fax	(01) 492 4770
E-mail	library@ireland.anglican.org.
Website address	www.library.ireland.anglican.org
Enquiries to	The Librarian and Archivist
Opening hours and facilities	9.30–1.00, 2.00–5.00, Mon–Fri; photocopying; photography and microfilming by arrangement
Guides	J.B. Leslie, *Catalogue of manuscripts in possession of the Representative Church Body* (1938); Geraldine Fitzgerald, 'Manuscripts in the Representative Church Body Library', *Analecta Hibernica* 23 (1966); Raymond Refaussé, 'The Representative Church Body Library and the records of the Church of Ireland', *Archivium Hibernicum* 49 (1995); Raymond Refaussé, *Church of Ireland records* (1999); Report of the Library and Archives Committee, containing an annual accessions list, is published annually in the *Journal of the General Synod of the Church of Ireland*

Major collections

Church of Ireland archives mainly from the Republic of Ireland: records of over 830 parishes, mainly in Counties Carlow, Clare, Cork, Dublin, Galway, Kerry, Kildare, Kilkenny, Mayo, Meath, Westmeath and Wicklow, early 17th century–; records of 17 dioceses, especially Cloyne, Dublin, Glendalough & Kildare, Ossory, Ferns & Leighlin, Meath and Tuam, late 13th century–; records of 17 cathedrals, especially Christ Church and St Patrick's, Dublin, St Canice's, Kilkenny, and St Brigid's, Kildare, early 14th century–; records of the General Synod and the Representative Church Body, 1870–.

Records of societies and organizations related to the Church of Ireland: schools, educational societies, missionary organizations, clerical groups, 18th–21st century.

Miscellaneous ecclesiastical manuscripts: papers of bishops, clergy and laity, correspondence, diaries, research notes and writings, scrapbooks, photographs; transcripts of non–extant Church of Ireland records, 17th–21st century.

Microfilms of Church of Ireland records, 17th–20th century, in other custodies.

Photographic archive mainly of church buildings but also of clergy, laity and church plate.

Oral history archive of recordings of bishops, clergy and laity, 20th century–.

193   Rockwell College

Address	Cashel County Tipperary
Telephone	((062) 61444
Fax	((062) 61661
E-mail	rockwell@iol.ie
Website address	www.rockwell-college.ie
Enquiries to	The Archivist
Opening hours and facilities	By appointment only; letter of recommendation required; fee payable for research visit

Major collections
Records of students and staff of the College, 1864–; photographs; Rockwell Annual, 1926–; College and Community journals, 1864–.

194   Roscommon County Council

Address	County Library Abbey Street Roscommon
Telephone	(0903) 37271/2/3/4/5/6/7
Fax	(0903) 25474
E-mail	roslib@iol.ie

Website address	http://ireland.iol.ie/~roslibl
Enquiries to	The County Librarian
Opening hours and facilities	1.00–8.00, Tue & Thur; 1.00–5.00, Wed; 10.00–1.00, 2.00–5.00, Fri & Sat; prior notice recommended; photocopying

Major collections

Athlone: No. 2 Rural District Council minutes, 1899–1925.

Boyle: Board of Guardian minutes, 1883–1920; Dispensary District minutes, 1852–96; Rural District Council minutes, 1896–9, and quarterly minutes, 1900–25.

Carrick-on-Shannon: Rural District Council minutes, 1903–16.

Castlerea: Board of Guardian minutes, 1839–1908; Rural District Council minutes: 1902–25.

Roscommon: Board of Health minutes: 1921–42; County Council minutes: 1899–; Grand Jury records, 1818–99; Pension Committee minutes, 1908–51; Board of Guardian minutes, 1884–1921; Rural District Council minutes, 1899–1926; Town Commissioners minutes, 1873–1910.

Strokestown: Board of Guardian minutes, 1850–1913; Rural District Council minutes, 1899–1921.

Papers of the Lloyd family of Croghan, 1660–1935; papers of the Gately family.

195   Royal College of Physicians of Ireland

Address	6 Kildare Street Dublin 2
Telephone	(01) 661 6677
Fax	(01) 676 3989
E-mail	robertmills@rcpi.ie
Website address	www.rcpi.ie
Enquiries to	The Librarian
Opening hours and facilities	9.30–1.00, 2.00–5.00, Mon–Fri appointment advisable; photocopying
Guides	Brian Donnelly, 'Records of the Royal College of Physicians', *Irish Archives* 1 (1989)

Major collections

Complete series of College minute books, 1692–; registers of fellows and members, late 17th century–; Committee proceedings books, 1828–; College correspondence, 1863–; administrative records relating to the Library, 19th century.

Medical and Philosophical Society minutes, 1756–84, 1856–1939.

Dublin Sanitary Association minutes, late 19th century.

National Association for the Prevention of Tuberculosis minutes, late 19th century.

Cow Pock Institution subscription book, 1804–43.

Indian Hospital case books, late 19th century.

Westmoreland Lock Hospital records, 1792–1922.

Sir Dominick Corrigan (1802–80): private papers.

Kirkpatrick biographical file: information on some 10,000 Irish medical practitioners.

Sir Patrick Dun's Hospital records, 1808–1986; St Ultan's Hospital records, 1919–84.

196   Royal College of Surgeons in Ireland

Address	The Widdess Room (Archives & Rare Books)
	The Mercer Library
	Mercer Street Lower
	Dublin 2
Telephone	(01) 402 2439
Fax	(01) 402 2457
E-mail	archivist@rcsi.ie
Website address	www.rcsi.ie
Enquiries to	The Archivist
Opening hours and facilities	9.00–5.00, Mon–Fri; appointment advisable; photocopying; photography
Guides	*Tracing medical ancestors* (Dublin, 2002).

Major collections

Records created by the Royal College of Surgeons in Ireland, 1784–.

Records created by other institutions. Mercer's Hospital (1734–1983): minute books of the governors 1736–; minute books of the medical board; clinical records of various departments of the hospital. House of Industry

Hospitals: minute books of the Corporation for relieving the poor in the County and City of Dublin, 1772–1871. Meath Hospital (founded 1753): sixteen volumes including governors' minute books, 1807–. Surgical Society of Ireland (1833–83): minutes of meetings of Council.

Records created by individuals associated with the history of medicine in Ireland including Richard Butcher, surgeon to Mercer's Hospital, case books, 1846–59; Charles A. Cameron, College historian, diaries, 1880–1916; Abraham Colles (1773–1843), surgeon, documentation relating to Colles; James A. Deeny (1906–94), former Chief Medical Adviser to the Irish Government, papers; William Doolin (1887–1962), surgeon and literary figure, papers; A. Jacob, President RCSI, 1837 and 1864, correspondence, 1840–3; Patrick Logan MD (d. 1988), chest physician and medical historian, papers; Bethel Solomons, gynaecologist, case books, 1914–21; L.B. Somerville-Large, ophthalmologist, case books, 1902–10; J.D.H. Widdess (1906–82), College librarian and historian, papers.

197   Royal Dublin Society

Address	Merrion Road Ballsbridge Dublin 4
Telephone	(01) 668 0866 ext. 288/240 7288
Fax	(01) 660 4014
E-mail	mary.kelleher@rds.ie
Enquiries to	The Librarian
Opening hours and facilities	10.00–5.00, Tue, Fri; 10.00–7.00, Wed, Thur; by appointment; photocopying

Major collections

Original minute books, 1731–64 (proceedings published from the minutes after 1764); Science Committee minute books, 1816–1979; Library Committee minute books, 1816–1984; Industries, Art and General Purposes Committee minute books, 1890–1917; Fine Arts Committee minute books, 1816–89.

Private paper collections of Professor George Fitzgerald (School of Engineering, Trinity College, Dublin), Dr Horace H. Poole, Richard M. Barrington and John Edmund Carew.

Records of the Radium Institute.

Photographic collection.

198   Royal Irish Academy

Address	19 Dawson Street Dublin 2
Telephone	(01) 676 2570/676 4222
Fax	(01) 676 2346
E-mail	library@ria.ie
Website address	www.ria.ie
Enquiries to	The Librarian
Opening hours and facilities	10.00–5.30, Mon–Thurs, 10.00–5.00, Fri; the Library is closed from three weeks from mid May to the end of the first week of June and for the last week in December; readers must complete a registration form (available on the RIA website) and produce a valid ID or letter of introduction from a member of the RIA or from a recognized institution; annual reader's tickets are issued for a fee of €12; the Library participates in the ALCID scheme; photocopying and microfilm printouts; photography and microfilming by arrangement
Guides	*Catalogue of Irish manuscripts in the Royal Irish Academy* (1926–70) 28 fascicules; Brigid Dolan, 'Genealogical sources at the Royal Irish Academy' in *Aspects of Irish genealogy* (1991); Elizabeth Fitzpatrick, *The catalogue of Irish manuscripts in the Royal Irish Academy: a brief introduction* (1988)

Major collections

Over 30 manuscripts pre-1600 including the Cathach or Psalter of St Columba (6th century); Domhnach Airgid (8th century); Stowe Missal (9th century); Lebor na hUidre (12th century); Book of Ballymote (14th century); Austin Friars Breviary, Book of Fermoy, Book of Hours, Book of Lecan, Leabhar Breac (15th century).

Major collection of *c.* 1,400 manuscripts in Irish, 17th–20th century, including the Hodges & Smith collection; the Betham, Hardiman, Hudson, O'Brien, O'Daly, O'Gorman and Reeves collections; the Stowe Irish manuscripts collection.

Antiquarian collections including the Hardiman and Windele papers; Ordnance Survey letters and memoirs; Gabriel Beranger watercolours; drawings of Dublin by George Petrie; topographical watercolours by

Richard Colt Hoare; Ordnance Survey sketches by George Victor du Noyer, George Petrie et al.; William Frederick Wakeman drawings.

Genealogical papers including those of Blackhall, De La Ponce, MacSwiney and Upton.

Natural history collections including those of A.H. Halliday, G.H. Kinahan, C. Longfield-Roberts, C.B. Moffatt, A.G. Moore, D.Y. Pack-Beresford, R.A. Phillips and R. Lloyd Praeger.

Papers of members of the RIA including O.J. Bergin, R. Day, Lord Charlemont and E. Knott.

Papers and diaries including those of C. Gavan Duffy, Katherine and Martha Wilmot.

Muniments of the RIA from its foundation in 1785.

199   Royal Irish Automobile Club

Address	34 Dawson Street Dublin 2
Telephone	(01) 677 5141
Fax	(01) 671 0793
E-mail	archive@motorsportireland.com
Website address	www.motorsportireland.com
Enquiries to	The Curator
Opening hours	By appointment; contact the Curator by post in advance

Major collections

The Guinness Segrave Library; photographs, films, video and automobilia relating to the history of motoring in Ireland

200   Royal Society of Antiquaries of Ireland

Address	63 Merrion Square Dublin 2
Telephone	(01) 676 1749
Fax	(01) 676 1749
E-mail	rsai@gofree.indigo.ie
Enquiries to	The Librarian

Opening hours and facilities	2.00–5.00, Mon–Fri; by appointment; photocopying
Guides	William Cotter Stubbs, 'The Weavers' Guild, the Guild of the Blessed Virgin Mary, Dublin 1446–1840', *Journal of Royal Society of Antiquaries of Ireland* 44, no. 1 (1919), 60–88

Major collections

Corporation books of Irish towns, especially from County Kilkenny; records of the Weavers' Guild of Dublin 1676–1840; archives of the RSAI, 1849–; a 13th-century illuminated Sarum missal; topographical drawings including 12 volumes of sketches by George Victor du Noyer and one volume by George Miller; sketches of Dublin by Brian Coghlan; notebooks of Patrick Joseph O'Reilly (1854–1924), including transcripts of 1642 depositions, and 23 volumes of pedigrees of the O'Reilly's; papers of Francis Elrington Ball, 1863–1928, historian and antiquary; and the papers of Lord Walter Fitzgerald, 1858–1923, soldier and antiquary, founder and editor of the *County Kildare Archaeological Society Journal.*

Large collection of 19th and early 20th century photographs especially of archaeological sites throughout Ireland: the main photographers are John L. Robinson, Ephraim MacDowel Cosgrave, Samuel K. Kirker, Thomas J. Westropp, Lord Walter Fitzgerald and Herbert T. Knox.

201   Royal Ulster Rifles Regimental Museum

Address	5 Waring Street Belfast BT I 2EW
Telephone	(02890) 232086
E-mail	rummuseum@yahoo.co.uk
Website address	http://rurmuseum.tripod.com
Enquiries to	The Honorary Curator
Opening hours and facilities	10–12.30, Mon–Thurs, 10.00–12.30, 2.00–3.00, Fri

Major collections

Officers' records of service, 83rd and 86th regiments, 19th century (microfilm); recruits' registers, 1924–39; unit war diaries, World War I and World War II; medal rolls; photograph albums and scrapbooks, 1900–; films.

202   RTÉ Sound Archives
Radio Telefis Éireann

Address   Radio Centre
                         Donnybrook
                         Dublin 4

Telephone   (01) 208 2044

Fax   (01) 208 2610

E–mail   sarchives@rte.ie

Website   www.rte.ie

Enquiries to   Sound Archives

Opening hours: 10.00–5.00, Mon–Fri; appointment necessary.
and facilities   Access charge applies; scale and conditions, including student rate, on application; academic research is limited to postgraduate level and higher; a full research, listening and copying service is available subject to copyright and other restrictions; copyright for much of the collections is held by RTÉ, other rights holders information available upon request. Copies cannot be provided without prior consent of copyright/rights holder in writing.

Major collections

RTÉ is the Irish National Public Service Broadcasting channel and is curator of the largest single collection of audio-visual archives in Ireland. RTÉ Sound Archive holds or has access to over 150,000 hours of programmes dating back to 1926 produced by four national radio stations. In the absence of a National Sound Archive, the RTÉ Sound Archives fulfills this role holding the audio history of the state with much of the collection comprising of news, current affairs, sport, music and other social, cultural and historical material. In addition to material produced by RTÉ, the collection also includes small deposits of locally produced or acquired interviews and recordings.

The collection comprises of material held on acetate disk, quarter-inch tape, cassette, CD-ROM, proprietary broadcast and other digital formats. Acquisition has increased in recent years with the Archives now acquiring c.28 hours of programmes from Radio One and 2FM each day.

Since 2000 a Radio Archive Project has been systematically transferring analogue recordings to internationally approved digital formats and ensuring that the legacy database records and current production records are standardized.

Access to parts of the collection is restricted for preservation and legal purposes. As the collection is the working archive of the national broadcaster and access facilities are limited, production requirements take precedence over external researchers.

203   RTÉ Television Archives
Radio Telefís Éireann

Address	Donnybrook Dublin 4
Telephone	(01) 208 3369/208 2786
Fax	(01) 208 3454
E-mail	archiveproject@rte.ie
Enquiries to	Library Sales
Opening Hours and facilities	9.15–1.00, 2.00–5–15 Mon–Fri; appointment necessary; a full research, viewing, and tape copying service is available, including telecine transfer; scale of charges is available upon request. RTÉ operates a special scale of charges for students at or above postgraduate level. Information is available on request from Library Sales. Copyright for much of the collections is held by RTÉ, other rights holders information available upon request. Copies cannot be provided without prior consent of copyright/rights holder in writing.

Major collections

RTÉ is the Irish National Public Service Broadcasting channel and is curator of the largest single collection of audio-visual archives in Ireland. Since the inauguration of television in 1961, the collection has grown to upwards of 160,000 hours of film and video content, comprising of news, current affairs, features, entertainment, drama and a wide variety of other television broadcast materials, as well as a large selection of stockshot material. Additionally there is a premier selection of Irish interest film material acquired from international news agencies and local sources dating from about 1913. There are also a growing number of smaller film and video collections deposited with RTE for preservation, restoration and digitisation from a variety of film and programme makers of the 20th century.

RTÉ TV Archives runs a dedicated restoration and conservation facility holding digital copies of valuable material and overseeing the restoration and transfer of media from vulnerable or obsolete formats to Digitalbeta tape. Film materials include 16mm film, b&w prints and negatives, 1962–74, and colour print and reversal, 1974–85. Records are accessible via computer database. A cataloguing project to standardise and update the legacy records and current production records has been ongoing since 2000. RTÉ News Library also provides daily up-to-date catalogue of all news material.

Access to parts of the collection is restricted for preservation and legal purposes. As the collection is the working archive of the national broadcaster, production requirements take precedence over external researchers.

204   RTÉ Stills Library
Radio Telefis Éireann

Address	Stills Library
	New Library Building
	Donnybrook
	Dublin 4
Telephone	(01) 208 3127
Fax	(01) 208 3031
ISDN	(01) 205 3350
E-mail	stillslibrary@rte.ie
Opening hours and facilities	9.15–5.30, Mon–Fri; appointment necessary CD-Rom, scanner, photographic printer, CD-burner, Zip-drive

Major collections

Radio Telefis Éireann (RTÉ) is the Irish National Public Service Broadcaster. A statutory corporation, it provides a comprehensive service on radio since 1926, and on television since 1961, and a large range of ancillary services. RTÉ Libraries, provide information and archive services to programme makers and corporate clients. The RTÉ Stills Library is one of a number of libraries in RTÉ. It currently holds a collection of approximately 110,000 digital images as well as some 300,000 images in original formats, covering a wide range of subjects relating to Irish life in the twentieth century. Original formats include glass plates (dating from the early 1900s), contact prints, negatives, 35mm and lantern slides and colour and black and white prints.

Cashman Collection: 669 photographs created by Joseph Cashman of Dublin, 1913–66. The photographs provide excellent coverage of political figures and events from a turbulent epoch in Irish history. The collection consists mainly of glass plates, many of which illustrate the 1916 Rising, the War of Independence and the Civil War.

Johnson Collection: 950 35mm negatives and contact prints taken by the English artist and photographer, Nevill Johnson, as a photographic record of Dublin City, 1952–53.

Murtagh Collection: *c.*397 photographs covering topics such as the 1916 Easter Rising, the burning of Cork city, the visit of George V to Ireland and the 1932 Eucharistic Congress.

Shard Collection (Cahill Collection): 500 images of a middle class family in south County Dublin/County Wicklow area at the turn of the 20th century. It is not certain whether the family is called Shard or whether Shard is the photographer or printer. It is also possible that a photographer named Cahill took these photographs. Hence the Shard collection is sometimes referred to as the Cahill collection.

Stills Department Collection: *c.*200,000 RTÉ copyright negatives and slides from the early years of RTÉ television to the end of 2001. The collection features stills from RTÉ television and radio programmes, and of Irish personalities and events. A selection of these images have been fully digitised and catalogued.

Access Magazine Collection: *c.*2,000 hard copy prints of images previously used in *Access*, the RTE staff magazine. Many of the prints were produced from negatives already held in the Stills Department Collection.

205   Society of the Sacred Heart of Jesus

Address	Provincial Archives
	Mount Anville Road
	Dublin 14
Telephone	(01) 278 0610
Fax	(01) 278 2557
Enquiries to	The Archivist

Opening hours and facilities	By appointment; photocopying and scanning
Guides	Survey list in Maria Duddy (ed.), *A directory for women's history in Ireland* (2000)

Major collections
Archives relating to the foundation, development and administration of houses and schools in the Irish/Scottish province and to provincial administration; archives relating to the foundation, development and administration of foreign missions in Uganda; records pertaining to religious; personal papers of religious, 1800–

206 St Columb's Cathedral

Address	London Street Londonderry
Telephone	(02871) 267313
Enquiries to	The Tourist Guide
Opening hours and facilities	9.00–1.00, 2.00–4.00, Mon–Sat, winter; 9.00–5.00, Mon–Sat, summer

Major collections
Cathedral and parish records, 1642–.
Munn Collection: 32 volumes of copies of records relating to the history of the City and County of Londonderry, 17th–19th century.
Tenison Groves Collection: copies of records relating to Londonderry including valuable information on the history of the London Companies, 17th century–.

207 St Columba's College

Address	Whitechurch Dublin 16
Telephone	(01) 490 6791
Fax	(01) 493 6655
E-mail	admin@stcolumbas.ie

Enquiries to	The Warden
Opening hours and facilities	By appointment

Major collections

Records relating to the administration of the College: College Register (record of entrances), 1843–, the year of foundation; minutes of the Fellows' meetings, 1890s–; minutes of Convention (staff meetings); accounts; pupils' reports.

Miscellaneous printed material relating to the foundation and history of the College including files of *The Columban,* 1879–, and the *Old Columban Bulletin*, 1950–.

Collection of photographs dating from 1859.

Founders' correspondence, 1841–2; letters from Dr J.H. Todd to Archbishop Lord John George Beresford, 1843; reminiscences of Revd William Sewell (1804–79), 1866.

Literary manuscripts; *The Lake Isle of Innisfree* presented by W.B. Yeats in 1936; *Museum* by Æ (George Russell); *In Exile* by Monk Gibbon; extract from *A Life* by Sir Dermot Boyle; two poems by Michael Ó Siadhail, 1991; and autographs of Douglas Hyde, Robin Flower and L.A.G. Strong.

A French Book of Hours, mid-14th century.

Correspondence relating to the Mioseach, a medieval Irish book shrine, 1843–.

208   St Columban's Missionary Society

Address	St Columban's Grange Road Donaghmede Dublin 13
Telephone	(01) 847 6647
Fax	(01) 848 4025
Enquiries to	The Archivist
Opening hours and facilities	10.00–5.00, Mon–Fri; by appointment; photocopying

Major collections

Correspondence relating to the foundation and development of the Society in China and the other countries where it is represented, 1912–.

209 St Finian's College

Address   Mullingar
                   County Westmeath

Telephone   (044) 48672

Fax   (044) 45275

Enquiries to   The President

Opening hours   By appointment; photocopying
and facilities

Major collections
College papers: accounts, student lists, examination results, photographs,
    19th–20th century.
Papers of Fr John Brady, diocesan historian, 1930s–60s; papers of Fr
    Michael McManus, mostly relating to the 1798 Rebellion in Counties
    Meath, Westmeath and Kildare, 1920s–70s.

210 St Kieran's College, Kilkenny

Address   St Kieran's College
                   Kilkenny

Telephone   (056) 21086

Fax   (056) 70001

E-mail   skc1728@iol.ie

Enquiries to   The Archivist

Opening hours   By appointment; photocopying
and facilities

Major collections
Carrigan and Graves MSS; collections of local interest compiled by priests
    of the diocese including Fr Moore, Healy, Clohessy and Dowling.
Research notes on College history; College account books, 1811–; index
    of students, 1782–1950; photographs and maps.

211 St Louis' Sisters

Address   St Louis' Convent
                   Monaghan
                   County Monaghan

Telephone   (047) 38931

E-mail   STLOUISARCHIVES@EIRCOM.NET

Enquiries to   The Archivist

Opening hours   By appointment
and facilities

Major collections
Material relating to the history of the Institute: property, administration,
   personnel, necrology, legal matters, foundations, ministries, publications,
   mid-19th century–

212 St Malachy's College, Belfast

Address   36 Antrim Road
                   Belfast BT15 2AE

Telephone   (02890) 74828

Fax   (02890) 741066

E-mail   stmalachys@campus.bt.com

Website address www.stmalachyscollege.com

Enquiries to   The Archivist

Opening hours   By appointment; photocopying
and facilities

Major collections
Archives of the College including lists of former students, *c.*1856–1926;
   account books, *c.*1844–; memoirs, diaries and photographs.
O'Laverty MSS: 16 Gaelic manuscripts acquired by Monsignor James
   O'Laverty PP, Holywood, County Down (d. 1906), historian of the dio-
   cese of Down and Connor; also available on microfilm in the National
   Library (q.v.).

Donnellan MSS: 2 Gaelic manuscripts from the South Armagh/North Louth
region, collected by the Revd L. Donnellan PP, County Armagh.
Correspondence of Muiris Ó Droighneáin, Gaelic scholar and former head
of Irish at St Malachy's, relating mainly to literary matters, c.1930–65.
Cuttings of books and fragmentary notes of Laurence O'Neill, lord mayor
of Dublin, c.1918–24.

213 St Mary's University College

Address	191 Falls Road Belfast BT12 6FE
Telephone	(02890) 276678
Fax	(02890) 333719
E-mail	j.morrissey@stmarys-belfast.ac.uk
Website address	www.stmarys-belfast.ac.uk
Enquiries to	The Librarian
Opening hours and facilities	9.00–9.00, Mon–Thurs, 9.00–5.00, Fri, 9.00–1.00, Sat (term), 9.00–5.00, Mon–Fri (vacation); appointment required

Major collections
Archives relating to the history and development of the College. Magee collection.

214 St Patrick's, Carlow College

Address	College Street Carlow
Telephone	(059) 913 1114
Fax	(059) 914 0258
E-mail	info@carlow.iecollege
Website address	www.carlowcollege.ie
Enquiries to	The Archivist

Opening hours   By appointment only; photocopying
and facilities

Major collections
The archives house part of the College Library collection, particularly materials relating to Bishops of Kildare and Leighlin, to diocesan history, and
to notable past students of Carlow College.
Microfilmed account books can be consulted at the National Library, Dublin
(q.v.); this is the main source on early students of the College, 1793–.

215   St Patrick's College, Cavan

Address	The Bishop's Residence
	Cullies
	Cavan
Telephone	(049) 433 1496
Fax	(049) 436 1796
E-mail	kilmorediocese@eircom.net
Website address	www.kilmorediocese.ie
Enquiries to	The Archivist
Opening houry	By appointment
and facilities	

Major collections
Archives of the College including rolls, prize lists, deeds, plans and account
books, 1839–.

216   St Patrick's College of Education

Address	Drumcondra
	Dublin 9
Telephone	(01) 884 2006
Fax	(01) 836 7613
Enquiries to	The President's Office

Opening hours By appointment
and facilities

Major collections
Archives of the College as an institution for the training of primary teachers. The material, which is not extensive, is partially catalogued.

217 St Patrick's College, Maynooth

Address Maynooth
County Kildare

Telephone (01) 628 5222

Fax (01) 628 9063

Enquiries to The College Archivist or Librarian, Russell Library

Opening hours 10.00–1.00, 2.00–5.00 Mon–Thurs; by appointment;
and facilities photocopying, photography, microfilm

Major collections
Archives of the College, 1795–.
Archives of the Irish College at Salamanca and other Irish colleges in Spain;
*c.*50,000 documents, 1592–1936.

St Patrick's College, Maynooth *see also* National University of Ireland, Maynooth

218 St Patrick's College, Thurles

Address Thurles
County Tipperary

Telephone (0504) 21201/24466

Fax (0504) 23735

E-mail luceaet@eircom.net

Enquiries to The Archivist

Opening hours　By appointment; photocopying
and facilities

Major collections
Much of the College archives relates to College administration since its
　foundation in 1837 and is pastorally privileged, confidential and inac-
　cessible. Basic biographical information on past students is available as
　well as considerable material on day to day expenses and property.
Papers of Fr Michael Maher containing biographical material on former
　clergy of the archdiocese of Cashel and Emly and material relevant to
　parochial histories of the archdiocese. Includes a diary commenting upon
　contemporary ecclesiastical and civil events with particular reference to
　the War of Independence.
Parochial register for the parish of Boherlahan, 1736–40.

219　　St Patrick's Hospital

Address　　　Steeven's Lane
　　　　　　　James's Street
　　　　　　　Dublin 8

Telephone　　(01) 249 3200

Enquiries to　The Chief Executive Officer/Medical Director

Opening hours　By appointment only
and facilities

Major collections
Records from the foundation of the hospital in 1745 up to the present day
　including the following:
Records relating to the general administration of the hospital. Among the
　most significant of these are a complete set of minute book of the Board
　of Governors from the foundation of the hospital; foundation charter and
　subsequent supplemental charters; reports of government inspectors on
　the hospital from the late 19th and early 20th centuries; records relating
　to some of the masters or medical superintendents of the hospital, espe-
　cially Dr Richard Leeper (medical superintendent, 1899–1942).
Records relating to the hospital's finances and property including petitions
　to parliament for funding, 1755 & 1757; patient accounts, late 19th cen-
　tury; maps, correspondence, rentals and legal records relating to estates

owned by the hospital in Dublin, Ferns and Saggart, mid-18th century–.

Records relating to patients including admission records, 1841–; registers of patients, 1795–; medical records, 1845–; reports and statistical information on patients, mainly 20th century.

Financial and legal papers concerning the final years of Jonathan Swift and the administration of his estate in relation to the foundation of the hospital including records of the committee of guardians appointed to administer Swift's affairs in the last years of his life; records relating to Swift's funeral; records created by the trustees appointed under the terms of Swift's will to found the hospital.

Records relating to the hospital buildings including the original plans and specifications for the building by the architect, George Semple, 1749; plans of later additions and refurbishments; plans for a district lunatic asylum submitted to the hospital by the architect, Francis Johnston.

Records documenting the history of St Edmundsbury, a convalescent branch of the hospital which was established in Lucan in 1899, including a survey of the estate of Agmondisham Vesey of 1772 incorporating a survey of the St Edmundsbury estate.

220   St Peter's College

Address	Summerhill Wexford
Telephone	(053) 45111/42071/45511
Fax	(053) 45111
E-mail	whowell@gofree.indigo.ie
Enquiries to	Ferns Diocesan Centre, St Peter's College
Opening hours and facilities	By appointment; photocopying

Major collections
Hore Manuscripts relating to the history of Wexford, *c.*1798.
Material relating to the development of St Peter's College, 1811–.
Material relating to the diocese of Ferns.
Papers of the Revd T. O'Byrne, G. Flood and R. Ranson.

221 Servite Fathers
(Order of Friar Servants of Mary)

Address	Servite Priory
	Benburb
	Dungannon
	County Tyrone
Telephone	(02837) 548241
Enquiries to	The Archivist
Opening hours and facilities	Postal enquiry; photocopying

Major collections
Material relating mainly to the Order in Ireland including the foundation
  years, 1947–, with some material relating to the Order worldwide.

222 Sisters of Charity

Address	Religious Sisters of Charity Generalate
	Caritas
	15 Gilford Road
	Sandymount
	Dublin 4
Telephone	(01) 269 7833
Fax	(01) 260 3085
Enquiries to	The Archivist
Opening hours and facilities	By appointment only; letter of recommendation required for first time researchers; photocopying

Major collections
Material relating to the life and work of the Sisters of Charity from their
  foundation in 1815. The largest collections relates to the foundress, Mary
  Aikenhead, and there is also a substantial body of material relating to
  Mother Arsenius Morrough-Bernard and the Providence Woollen Mills
  which she established in Foxford, County Mayo, to provide employment
  for local people.

Sisters of Mercy *see* **Mercy Congregational Archives**

223   Sisters of St Claire

Address   91 Harold's Cross Road
Dublin 6W

E-mail   stclare@eircom.net

Enquiries to   The Archivist

Opening hours   Postal enquiries only
and facilities

Major collections
Material relating to the history of the Order, and work, since 1629, in Ireland.

224   Sisters of St Claire

Address   High Street
Newry
County Down BT34 1HD

Enquiries to   The Archivist

Opening hours   Postal enquiries only
and facilities

Major collections
Material relating to the history of the Order, and work, since 1629, in Ireland.

225   Sligo Borough Council

Address   City Hall
Quay Street
Sligo

Telephone   (071) 42141

Enquiries to	The Town Clerk
Opening hours and facilities	9.00–1.00, 2.00–5.00, Mon–Fri

Major collections

Minutes of Sligo Corporation meetings, 1842–1991; register of premises (Explosives Act, 1875), 1879–1916; register of music performed in the Town Hall, 1938–46; register of public entertainments (Town Hall), 1930–48; minutes of artisans & housing committees, 1886–1920; lists of burgesses of Sligo Borough, 1868–1906; Sligo Cemetery Trust ledger, 1868–86; valuation & rate books, 1842–.

226   Sligo County Library

Address	Sligo County Library Headquarters The Westward Town Centre Bridge Street Sligo
Telephone	(071) 914 7190
Fax	(071) 914 6798
E-mail	sligolib@sligococo.ie
Enquiries to	The County Librarian
Opening hours and facilities	10.00–12.54, 2.00–4.45 Mon–Fri; photocopying
Guides	*Sligo: Sources of Local History* (1988)

Major collections

Minute books of Board of Guardians, 1850–90; Grand Jury Presentments minute books, 1813–51, 1877–99; Sligo County Council minute books, 1899–1950.

J.C. McDonagh MSS relating to County Sligo (22 vols).

Rentals of Palmerston Estate, 1860, 1879, 1888, 1902.

Pedigrees of various county families.

Drawings of antiquities of County Sligo by W.F. Wakeman.

227   Sligo Harbour Commissioners

Address	Harbour Office Ballast Quay Sligo
Telephone	(071) 61197
Fax	(071) 61197
Enquiries to	The Secretary
Opening hours and facilities	9.00–5.00, Mon–Fri

Major collections

Minute books, 1824–8, 1847–; memoranda of agreements book, 1823–92; miscellaneous accounts and operational books, late 19th century–; report on improvements to harbour, 1822.

228   Society of African Missions

Address	Blackrock Road Cork
Telephone	(021) 292871
Fax	(021) 293876
E-mail	smarchives@oceanfree.net
Enquiries to	The Archivist
Opening hours and facilities	By appointment

Major collections

Correspondence and papers of the Irish Province of the Society from 1885 to the present day including material relating to the administration of the Irish houses of the Province and the Province's Missions in Liberia, Nigeria, Tanzania, Zambia, South Africa, Australia and South America: *coutumiers*, diaries and memoirs; material on the individual jurisdictions staffed by the Society; biographical material on members of the Province.
Kevin Carroll photographic collection: African arts and crafts, 1940–70.

229 Society of St Vincent de Paul

Address	8 New Cabra Road Dublin 7
Telephone	(01) 838 4164/7
Fax	(01) 838 7355
E-mail	info@svp.ie
Website address	www.svp.ie
Enquiries to	The National Secretary
Opening hours and facilities	9.30–5.30, Mon–Fri, by appointment

Major collections

Records of the Society, 1833–; material relating to the founder, Frederic Ozanam, and to St Vincent de Paul; copies of the Society's *Bulletin*.

230 South Eastern Education and Library Board

Address	Library Headquarters Windmill Hill Ballynahinch County Down BT24 8DH
Telephone	(02897) 566400
Fax	(02897) 565072
E-mail	ref@bhinchlibhq.demon.co.uk
Website address	www.seelb.org.uk
Enquiries to	The Principal Assistant Librarian, Irish and Local Studies
Opening hours and facilities	9.00–5.00, Mon–Fri; telephone in advance for an appointment if possible

Major collections

Material relating to travel and literature in County Down.
Collections of photographs and postcards.

231 Southern Education and Library Board

Address   Irish and Local Studies Library
39c Abbey Street
Armagh BT61 7EB

Telephone   (02837) 27851

Fax   (02837) 52712

Enquiries to   The Irish and Local Studies Librarian

Opening hours 9.30–1.00, 2.00–5.00, Mon, Wed and Fri; 2.00–500, Tue,
and facilities   9.30–1.00, 2.00–8.00, Thurs

Major collections

Croslé papers relating to the history of Newry and district.

Southern Education and Library Board annual reports and minutes, 1973–.

Armagh, Banbridge, Cookstown and Newry Board of Guardians minutes (microfilm).

Armagh County Council minutes, 1937–73; Armagh County Library Committee minutes, 1928–72; Armagh City and District Council minutes, 1984–.

Banbridge Urban District Council minutes, 1973–86; Cookstown District Council minutes, 1975–85; Craigavon District Council minutes, 1973–85; Craigavon Arts Committee minutes, 1981–91; Dungannon District Council minutes, 1973–85; Newry and Mourne District Council minutes, 1973–81; Portadown Urban District Council minutes, 1948–63;

232 Stranmillis University College: a College of The Queen's University of Belfast

Address   Stranmillis Road
Belfast BT9 5DY

Telephone   (02890) 384310

Fax   (02890) 663682

E-mail   Library@Stran.ac.uk

Enquiries to   The Librarian

Opening hours and facilities	Term, 9.00–9.00, Mon–Thurs; 9.00–4.30, Fri; 9.00–1.00, Sat; vacation, 9.00–5.00, Mon–Thurs; 9.00–4.30, Fri; photocopying

Major collections
Documentary and photographic records of the College and grounds since its establishment in 1922. Also prospectuses and other printed ephemera.

233   Temple House

Address	Ballymote County Sligo
Telephone	(071) 83329
Fax	(071) 83808
E-mail	guests@templehouse.ie
Website	www.templehouse.ie/
Enquiries to	The Proprietor
Opening hours and facilities	By appointment

Major collections
Papers of the Perceval family and of the related Metcalfe, Bayley, de Hamel and Blane families, mostly 1864–, with some earlier material.

234   Tipperary Joint Libraries

Address	Castle Avenue Thurles County Tipperary
Telephone	(0504) 21555/21154/21102/21156
Fax	(0504) 23442
E-mail	studies@tipperearylibraries.ie
Website address	www.tipperarylibraries.ie
Enquiries to	Local Studies Department

Opening hours and facilities	9.30–5.30, Mon–Fri; photocopying
Guides	Introductory leaflet available in branch libraries

Major collections

Poor Law Union records: Borrisokane, 1850–1925; Cashel, 1844–1925; Clogheen, 1839–1929; Clonmel, 1839–1924; Nenagh, 1839–1924; Roscrea, 1839–1924; Thurles, 1839–1924; Tipperary, 1839–1923.

Presentments to the Grand Juries of Tipperary, 1842–99.

Rentals, maps, schedules relating to the sale of encumbered estates: lands in the barony of Slieveardagh/Comsy, 1851; estates of the Earl of Portarlington at Borrisoleigh, 1855 and Roscrea, 1858; estate of Viscount Chabot at Thurles and Thomastown, 1859.

Family papers: Coopers of Killenure, 1879–98; Ryans of Inch, 1650–1928.

235   South Tipperary County Museum

Address	Mick Delahunty Square Clonmel
Telephone	(052) 34500
Fax	(052) 80390
E-mail	museum@southtippcoco.ie
Enquiries to	The Curator/Document Assistant
Opening hours and facilities	10.00–5.00, Tue–Sat; photocopying
Guides	An introductory leaflet and a series of interpretative lists and hand lists are available

Major collections

The County Museum holds archival material relating to local authorities in the county. It includes the minute books of Tipperary S.R. County Council, 1899–1952, and of various Council committees as well as the minute books of Fethard Town Commissioners, 1866–77, 1896–1929. The collections also include material relating to the Lismore estate and the records of the Republican Courts in the eastern part of the county during the War of Independence, for which three days notice is required.

236 Trinity College, Dublin Geological Museum

Address	Geological Museum Department of Geology Trinity College Dublin 2
Telephone	(01) 608 1477
Fax	(01) 671 1199
E-mail	wysjcknp@tcd.ie
Enquiries to	The Curator
Opening hours and facilities	10.00–4.30, Mon–Fri; groups by appointment; photocopying; photography
Guides	P.N. Wyse Jackson, 'Museum File 18: Geological Museum, Trinity College, Dublin', *Geology Today* 6 (1989), 213–14; P.N. Wyse Jackson, 'The Geological Collections of Trinity College, Dublin', *Geological Curator* 5, no. 7 (1992), 263–74.

Major collections

Charlesworth, Edward (1813–93): catalogue of specimens sent to Professor Oldham *c.*1848.

Geological Society of Dublin/Royal Geological Society of Ireland: minute books and other manuscript items (detailed by Davies 1965). Graydon, Revd George (d. 1803), cleric: diary of travels in Northern Italy (*c.*1792); catalogue of volcanic products collected in Italy. Griffith, Sir Richard (1784–1878), geologist and public servant: manuscript catalogue of carboniferous fossils presented to the Dublin University Museum (1844).

Hudson, R.G.S. (1895–1965), geologist: correspondence. Joly, John (1857–1933), geologist: diaries, manuscripts, research notebooks, and catalogue of mineral collection.

Knox, Hon. George (1765–1827), Parliamentarian: three catalogues of minerals, some of which are now in TCD.

Leskean collection: manuscript entitled 'Synopsis of the arrangement of the Vulcanic Cabinet annexed to the Leskean Collection in the Museum of the Dublin Society', written on paper, watermark dated 1804. This collection was acquired by the Dublin Society in 1792 and is now in the National Museum of Ireland.

Mallett, Robert (1810–81), civil engineer, seismologist: catalogue of volcanic products collected in Italy in 1864 and 1869.

Perceval, Robert, professor of Chemistry, TCD: catalogue of minerals *(c.* 1803).

Ryan, James: Geological report on Isabella Pit, Workington (*c.*1798).

Smyth, Louis Bouvier (1893–1953), geologist: correspondence, laboratory notebooks, field notebooks, field maps.

Sollas, William Johnson (1849–1936), geologist: letter relating to Piltdown Man.

237   Trinity College Library, Dublin Manuscripts Department

Address	College Street Dublin 2
Telephone	(01) 608 1189
Fax	(01) 608 2690
E-mail	mscripts@tcd.ie
Website address	www.tcd.ie/Library/
Enquiries to	The Keeper of Manuscripts
Opening hours and facilities	10.00–5.00, Mon–Fri, I0.00–1.00, Sat; photography; microfilming
Guides	T.K. Abbott, *Catalogue of the manuscripts in the Library of Trinity College, Dublin* (1900) is a general catalogue of accessions to 1900, continued after that date in type-script form. Introductory leaflet to the department is available throughout the Library. Sectional language catalogues have appeared in print, including T.K. Abbott and E.J. Gwynn, *Catalogue of the Irish manuscripts in the Library of Trinity College, Dublin* (1921); Marvin L. Colker, *A descriptive catalogue of the mediaeval and Renaissance Latin manuscripts in the Library of Trinity College Dublin* (1991). Peter Fox (ed.), *Treasures of the Library, Trinity College Dublin* (1986) discusses some of the major holdings.

Major collections

Corpus of medieval manuscripts, largely from the collection of James Ussher (d. 1656), but also including the Library's greatest treasures: the Book of

Kells (c.800), Book of Durrow (c.675), Book of Armagh (807), Book of Dimma (8th century), Book of Mulling (8th century), Matthew Paris's life of St Alban (13th century), Fagel Missal (15th century).

College muniments, 16th–21st century; Roman inquisitorial records, 16th–18th century; Depositions of 1641; 1798 rebellion papers; archives of the Royal Zoological Society of Ireland, 1836–c.1953.

Family and private paper collections of William King (1650–1729), archbishop of Dublin; Thomas Parnell (1679–1718), poet; Earls of Donoughmore, 16th–20th century; Wynne family of Hazlewood, County Sligo and Glendalough, County Wicklow, 18th–20th century; Elvery family of Carrickmines and Foxrock, County Dublin, 19th–20th century; Sir William Rowan Hamilton (1805–65), mathematician and astronomer; Michael Davitt (1846–1906), author and politician; John Dillon (1851–1927), politician; Robert Erskine Childers (1870–1922), author and politician; Liam de Róiste (1882–1959), politician and author; John Millington Synge (1871–1909), poet and dramatist; Susan Mitchell (1866–1926), poet and editor; Thomas Bodkin (1887–1961), art historian and gallery director; Thomas MacGreevy (1893–1967), poet and gallery director; Denis Johnston (1901–84), playwright and journalist; Frank Gallagher (1893–1962), journalist; Joseph Campbell (1876–1944), poet; James Stephens (1880–1950), author; Martin Ó Cadhain (1905–70), writer in Irish; George McBeth (1932–93), poet and novelist; John Banville (b. 1945), novelist; Samuel Beckett (1906–89), author; Hubert Butler (1900–90), essayist; Gerald Barry (born 1952), composer; John B. Keane (b. 1928–2003), author; Gerald Victory (1921–95), composer and broadcaster; Noel Browne (1915–97), doctor, social reformer and politician; Jennifer Johnston (b. 1920), novelist and playwright; Tom Murphy (b. 1925), playwright; Pike Theatre, 1950s–1960s.

238 Ulster Folk and Transport Museum Library

Address Cultra Manor
Holywood
County Down BT18 0EU

Telephone (02890) 428428

Fax (02890) 428728

E-mail uftm@nidex.com

Website address	www.nidex.com/uftm/index.htm
Enquiries to	The Librarian
Opening hours and facilities	9.00–1.00, 2.00–5.00, Mon–Fri; appointment preferred photocopying; photography
Guides	M. McCavana and G. Loughran, *The B.B.C. Radio Archive catalogue for Northern Ireland* (1992)

Major collections

Byers folklore collection, *c.*1900; Committee on Ulster Folklife and Traditions notebooks, *c.*1960; Huddleston vernacular poetry collection, *c.*1830–80; Ulster Dialect Dictionary collection.

Living Linen archive of recordings of people associated with the linen industry.

W.A. Green photographic collection; Harland & Wolff photographic collection.

British Broadcasting Corporation archive: radio programmes since the inception of the BBC in Northern Ireland in 1924 but most of the material is from the 1960s onwards; film archive from the 1950s but mostly from the 1960s.

239   Ulster Museum

Address	Botanic Gardens Belfast BT9 5AB
Telephone	(02890) 383000
Fax	(02890) 383013
E-mail	history.um@nics.gov.uk
Enquiries to	The Department of History
Opening hours and facilities	10.00–12.30, 2.00–4.00, Mon–Fri; prior appointment only; photocopying; photography
Guides	*Concise catalogue of the drawings, paintings & sculptures in the Ulster Museum* (1986); N. Fisher, 'George Crawford Hyndman's MSS', *Journal of Conchology* 19 (1931), 164; B.S. Turner and others, *A list of the photographs in the R.J. Welch Collection in the Ulster Museum,* 1: *topography and history* (Ulster Museum, 1979); 2: *botany, geology and zoology* (Ulster Museum, 1983).

Major collections

Templeton MSS: *c.*25 vols of MSS of John Templeton (1766–1825), botanist; including his journal, 1806–25, several volumes of an unpublished Irish flora illustrated by himself, records of mosses and ferns and a list of Irish shells.

Hyndman MSS: numerous notes by George C. Hyndman (1796–1868), Belfast marine biologist; also dredging papers, Belfast Bay, 1844–57.

Thompson MSS: several folders of notes and correspondence of William Thompson (1805–52), Belfast naturalist and author of *Natural history of Ireland.*

Welch MSS: *c.*20 vols of personal and excursion diaries, natural history notes, memoranda and lists of negatives of Robert J. Welch (1859–1936), photographer and amateur naturalist.

Botany and Zoology Department: small but important collections, including notebooks of P.H. Grierson (1859–1952) on Mollusca and one letter of Dr Alexander Henry Halliday (?1728–1802) relating to Insecta.

Local History Department: extensive archive of manuscript and printed material, including the Barber MSS (Revd Samuel Barber of Rathfriland, United Irishman) and the Tennant Collection (Robert J. Tennant, early 19th-century Liberal politician from Belfast).

Non-manuscript material: posters and other ephemera, chiefly playbills and programmes of Belfast theatres (*c.*200–250 items).

Belfast and other locally printed books, pamphlets, chapbooks and broadsides (*c.*500 items).

Hogg Collection: approx. 5,500 glass plate negatives plus many lantern slides, by A.R. Hogg of Belfast (1870–1939), covering topography, industry, commerce, social conditions and portraits.

Welch Collection: *c.*6,000 glass plate negatives by R.J. Welch of Irish subjects, covering topography, industries, rural crafts, antiquities, geology, botany and zoology.

Historical and Topographic Collection: *c.*1,000 negatives, modern and copied from old prints and negatives (constantly growing); a few other collections, large and medium-sized (uncatalogued or in process of being catalogued).

A growing collection of several hundred slides made in the field and from specimens and photographs.

Departments other than Local History keep their own specialized collections of negatives and slides.

Local History Department: *c.*250 maps; *c.*1,500 topographical drawings, paintings and prints; *c.*250 portraits.

Art Department: *c.*2,000 drawings and watercolors.

Botany and Zoology Department: various watercolours and drawings.

240   Ulster Television Film Library

Address	Havelock House Ormeau Road Belfast BT7 1EB
Telephone	(02890) 328122
Fax	(02890) 246695
E-mail	wgarrett@utvplc.com
Website address	u.tv
Enquiries to	Archives Supervisor at (02890) 2144
Opening hours	By appointment or postal enquiry

Major collections
Most programmes produced by Ulster Television, 1957–.
Film and VTR record of most major events in Northern Ireland, 1957–.

241   Unitarian Church

Address	112 St Stephen's Green Dublin 2
Enquiries to	The Secretary
Opening hours and facilities	By appointment only

Major collections
Records of Eustace Street (formerly New Row), Cook Street and St
   Stephen's Green (formerly Wood Street), Dublin, congregations, early
   18th century–.
Records of Cork (Princes Street) congregation, 1799–1844.
Irish Unitarian Christian Society: minutes, 1830–99.

University College Cork *see* National University of Ireland, Cork

242 University College Dublin Archives Department

Address:	Belfield, Dublin 4
Telephone:	(01) 716 7555
Fax:	(01) 716 1146
E-mail:	archives@ucd.ie
Website:	http://www.ucd.ie/~archives
Enquiries to:	Principal Archivist
Opening hours and facilities	10.00–1.00, 2.00–5.00, Mon–Thur; reader's ticket and appointment necessary; photocopying, photography, digital imaging

Major collections

Private paper collections relating to the movement for national independence and the political and cultural development of the modern Irish state. Major collections include papers of Frank Aiken, Todd Andrews, Kevin Barry, Ernest Blythe, Colonel Dan Bryan, Michael Collins, John A. Costello, Arthur Cox, Conor Cruise O'Brien, the Cumann na nGaedheal and Fine Gael Parties, the Fianna Fáil Party, Desmond FitzGerald, George Furlong, George Gavan Duffy, Michael Hayes, T.M. Healy, Sighle Humphreys, Hugh Kennedy, Tom Kettle, Denis McCullough, Sean MacEntee, Sean MacEoin, Patrick McGilligan, Mary MacSwiney, Terence MacSwiney, Con Moloney, Michael Moynihan, Richard Mulcahy, Donnchadh Ó Briain, Col. George O'Callaghan-Westropp, Daniel O'Connell, Kathleen O'Connell, Cearbhall Ó Dálaigh, Muiris Ó Droighneáin, Diarmuid Ó hEigeartaigh, Ernie O'Malley, Alfred O'Rahilly, The O'Rahilly, Desmond Ryan, Dr James Ryan, W.P. Ryan, Moss Twomey and Eamon de Valera.

Records of predecessor institutions of the university including the Catholic University of Ireland, 1854–1911; the Royal College of Science for Ireland, 1867–1926; the Museum of Irish Industry, 1846–47; Albert Agricultural College, 1838–1926; and the Royal Veterinary College of Ireland, 1900–60.

Records of student and alumni bodies including the Literary & Historical Society and the National University Women Graduates' Association.

Private paper collections of distinguished former members of the university and its predecessor bodies including papers of Timothy Corcoran SJ, T.W.T. Dillon, R. Dudley Edwards, Françoise Henry, Tom Kettle,

Roger McHugh, Eoin MacNeill, F.X. Martin, James Meenan, Eugene O'Curry, David James O'Donoghue, John Marcus O'Sullivan and Michael Tierney.

Collection of Gaelic manuscripts, designated 'A' MSS, 11th–20th centuries, formerly housed in the Franciscan Library Killiney and transferred to the custody of UCDAD under the terms of the OFM-UCD Partnership Agreement. Includes the Martyrology of Tallaght [fragment of the Book of Leinster], the Annals of the Four Masters, the Psalter of St Caimin and the Liber Hymnorum.

Family and estate paper collections, 17th century–, of the Bryan family (Dublin); Caulfield (Tyrone); de Clifford (Down); Delachirois (Down); Fitzpatrick (Laois); Hart-Synnot (Dublin); Herbert (Kerry); Hutchinson and Synge Hutchinson (Dublin and Wicklow); Potter (Down); Rice of Mountrice (Kildare); Upton (Westmeath and Louth); and Wandesford (Kilkenny).

Trade union archives and labour-related private paper collections deposited through the Irish Labour History Society. Includes archives of actors, bakers, coopers, municipal employees, plasterers, shoe and leather workers, and woodworkers trade unions.

243 University College Dublin Cartlann na gCanúintí

Address Áras J.H. Newman
An Coláiste Ollscoile
Baile Átha Cliath 4

Telephone (01) 716 8106

Fax (01) 269 4409

E-mail mgunn@ucd.ie

Enquiries to An Cartlannaí

Opening hours and facilities By appointment only; photocopying

Major collections

Established in 1953, Cartlann na gCanúintí includes amongst its holdings the original manuscripts of Tomás Ó Criomhthain *Stair na mBlascaodaí: Beag agus Mór*; Conchubhair Ó Síothcháin *Seanchas Chléire* (1940); William McLees's unpublished 12 volume English to Irish and Scottish Gaelic Dictionary (1953); the Dún Chaoin memoirs of Seán Ó Dálaigh;

the Cape Clear journals of Donnchadh S. Ó Drisceoil on which his regular Irish Times column was based and a selection of which became the book *Aistí ó Chléire* (1987).

Cartlann na gCanúintí's collection of *c*.400,000 dictionary entries held in card index format which have formed the basis of many general as well as academic reference dictionaries. Consists of entries compiled by the current archivist from seventeeth century manuscript materials, as well as original field collections compiled by twentieth century lexicographers including some of Ireland's most distinguished folklore collectors, writers and professional translators such as Seán Ó Ruadháin, Pilib Ó Foghludha, Seosamh Ó Dálaigh, Pádraig Ua Maoleoin. Séamas Ó Maolchathaigh *An Gleann agus a Raibh Ann* (1963), Tomás Laighléis *Seanchas Thomáis Laighléis* (1977).

Private and research papers and field notes of Tomás de Bhaldraithe, successively professor of Modern Irish Language and Literature and professor of Irish Dialectology in University College Dublin, including correspondence between poets, writers and scholars, leaders of the Irish language movement and other public figures such as Professor Cormac Ó Cadhla, Eric Mac Fhinn, Dónall Mac Amhlaigh, Tomás Ó Máille, Máirtín Ó Flaithbheartaigh, Mícheál Ó Maoláin, Eoin McKiernan, Colm Ó Gaora, Mícheál Ó Siochfhradha, Máire Mac an tSaoi, Máirtín Ó Direáin, Eibhlín Ní Bhriain and Seosamh Dáibhéid.

Audio tapes including field recordings made in the 1960s by Professor Hans Hartmann with accompanying correspondence and transcripts.

Concordances of many of the published works of Ó Cadhain, Ó Criomhthain, Ó Conaire, Mac Grianna, Ó Céileachair and others. Some digital and microform materials and rare books and journals, including a large collection of books presented by President de Valera in 1973 to Cartlann na gCanúintí to mark its twentieth anniversary.

244 University College Dublin Roinn Bhéaloideas Éireann/ Department of Irish Folklore

Address   Belfield
               Dublin 4

Telephone   (01) 706 8216/706 8327

Fax   (01) 706 1144

E-mail	hennigan@macollamh.ucd.ie
Enquiries to	Head of Department
Opening hours and facilities	2.30–5.30, Mon–Fri, excluding August; the Irish Folk Music section of the Department (UCD, Earlsfort Terrace) is open by appointment; photocopying; photography; microfilming
Guides	Seán O Súilleabháin, *A Handbook of Irish Folklore* (Dublin, 1942 and Detroit, 1970)

Major collections
Manuscripts, films, photographs, drawings and sound recordings held by the former Irish Folklore Commission (1935–71) as well as substantial additions, including video recordings, to these collections since 1971. The bulk of the manuscript holdings and sound and video recordings is in the Irish language, but these collections also contain large amounts of English-language material as well as smaller amounts of material in Scottish Gaelic and in the Manx and Breton languages.

245 University College Dublin Special Collections

Address	The Library University College Dublin Belfield Dublin 4
Telephone	(01) 716 7686/ 716 7149
E-mail	special.collections@ucd.ie
Website address	www.ucd.ie/library/collectiuons/specoll.html
Enquiries to	The Special Collections Librarian
Opening hours and facilities	10.00–1.00, 2.00–5.00, Mon–Fri; by appointment; photocopying; photography; microfilming by arrangement

Major collections
Some papers relating to the movement for national independence, Irish language and local history, and early 20th-century Anglo-Irish literature.

Includes letters and papers of and relating to Gerard Manley Hopkins (1845–89), James Joyce (1882–1941), Patrick Kavanagh (1904–67), Thomas Kettle (1880–1916), Henry Morris (Énrí Ó Muirgheasa) (1874–1945), John O'Donovan (1809–61), Seán Ó Ríordáin (1916–77), William Reeves (1815–92), Jack Butler Yeats (1871–1957); Mary Lavin (1912–96); novels and plays of Maeve Binchy; plays, poems and short stories of Frank McGuinness (1953–).

Minute books of the council of the Irish Academy of Letters, 1932–70.

University College Galway *see* National University of Ireland, Galway

246   University of Limerick

Address	Library & Information Service University of Limerick Limerick
Telephone	(061) 202690
Fax	(061) 202541
E-mail	specoll@ul.ie
Website address	www.ul.ie/rarebooks/
Enquiries to	The Special Collections Librarian
Opening hours and facilities	9.00–1.00, 2.15–5.00, Mon–Fri; appointment necessary; photocopying; photography; digital imaging by arrangement

Major collections

Private collections include the papers of Madge Daly, Jim Kemmy and Robert Stradling

Family and estate papers of the Earl of Dunraven (Limerick); the Knight of Glin (Limerick); Eyre Coote family (Laois and Dublin)

Literary collections of Edward P. McGrath, Kate O'Brien, J.M. Neill and Maurice Walsh

247   University of Ulster Library at Coleraine

Address	Coleraine County Londonderry BT52 1SA
Telephone	(04870) 400 700
Fax	(02870) 324357
Enquiries to	The Librarian
Opening hours and facilities	9.00–10.00, Mon–Fri, 10.0–5.00 Sat during term; 9.00–5.00 Mon–Fri during vacation; photocopying; photography by arrangement

Major collections
Papers of George Shiels (1881–1949), playwright; Denis Johnston (1901–84), playwright and author; John Hewitt (1907–87) poet, Francis Stuart (1902–), novelist; George Stelfox (1884–1972), naturalist; E. Norman Carrothers (1898–1977), botanist and railway engineer.
Headlam-Morley collection of World War I material.
Paul Ricard collection of World War II material.

248   University of Ulster Library at Magee College

Address	Magee College Northland Road Londonderry BT48 7JL
Telephone	(02871) 375264
Fax	(02871) 375626
E-mail	sa.mcmullan@uist.ac.uk
Website address	www.uist.ac.uk/library
Enquiries to	The Librarian
Opening hours and facilities	9.00–9.00, Mon–Fri, 10.00–1.00 Sat during term; 9.00–5.00, Mon–Fri during vacation; photocopying

Major collections
A small collection of manuscripts, mainly 18th- and 19th-century in origin, with an emphasis on sermons and Presbyterian history but including some items of a more general historical interest.

249   Valuation Office

Address	Block 2 Irish Life Centre Abbey Street Lower Dublin 1
Telephone	(01) 817 1000
Fax	(01) 817 1180
Enquiries to	The Secretary
Opening hours and facilities	9.30–12.30, 2.00–4.30, Mon–Fri; photocopying

Major collections
Griffith's Primary Valuation, *c*.1852, for the Republic of Ireland with accompanying maps. Records of the Valuation List, 1852–, showing occupiers of properties.

250   Vincentian Fathers (Congregation of the Mission) Irish Province

Address	Vincentian Provincial Office St Paul's Sybil Hill, Raheny Dublin 5
Fax	(01) 851 0846
E-mail	cmdublin@iol.ie
Enquiries to	The Archivist. First contact to be by letter, fax or e-mail.

Opening hours and facilities	By arrangement; photocopying
Guides	Thomas Davitt CM, 'The archives of the Irish Province of the Congregation of the Mission', *Catholic Archives* 5 (1985)

Major collections

Material relating to the history of Vincentians in Ireland, Britain, China and Nigeria; to personnel; to St Vincent de Paul; to the general history of the Vincentians and to prominent individual non–Irish Vincentians, 1833–. Includes manuscript and typescript accounts of persons, events and ministries; as well as theses, notebooks, sermon books, account books, correspondence and a collection of published books and pamphlets of Vincentian interest.

251   Waterford City Archives

Address	City Hall The Mall Waterford
Telephone	(051) 843123
Fax	(051) 879124
E-mail	archives@waterfordcity.ie
Website address	www.waterfordcity.ie/archives.php
Enquiries to	The City Archivist
Opening hours and facilities	By appointment; photocopying
Guides	*The royal charters of Waterford* (Waterford Corporation, 1992); Donal Moore, 'Waterford City Archives: a new service' in *Decies* 54; Donal Moore 'Sources for labour, social and economic history in Waterford City Archives' in *Saothar* 24 (1999)

Major collections

The Liber Antiquissimus, 1365–1649; the Scroll of Richard II, *c.*1390; the Royal Charters (20 items), 1449–1815; records of the Council, 1655–1992. Records of the Urban Sanitary Authority, 1874–1911; Waterford and New

Ross Port Sanitary Authority, 1904–49; Committees of the Corporation, 1778–1945; Town Clerk, 1377–1992; Engineer's Office, 1834–1960; Estate Office, 1700–1970, including expired leases, 1663–1970s; Finance Office, 1796–1958; Motor Tax Office, 1903–70s; Planning files, 1948–79; Housing survey, 1939.

Records of Waterford Chamber of Commerce, 1787–1997.

Small and private collections including Thomas Francis Meagher material, White's Chemist, Michael Walsh Asylum & Shea Institution, Waterford Music Club, Arts Advisory Committee, 1598–1980s.

Maps, plans and drawings, 1750s–1980s.

Photographs, 1870s–1990s.

Original data relating to archaelogical digs in the city, 1986–92.

252   Waterford County Archive Service

Address   Dungarvan Library Building
                        Davitt's Quay
                        Dungarvan
                        Waterford

Telephone   (058) 23673

E-mail   archivist@waterfordcoco.ie

Website address www.waterfordcoco.ie

Enquiries to   County Archivist

Opening hours   By appointment; photocopying
and facilities

Major collections

Archives of Waterford County Council, 1899–1960, and of predecessor bodies including the Grand Jury, 1829–99; Board of Guardians minute books for Waterford, 1848–1920, Lismore, 1843–1924, Dungarvan, 1849–1922, Kilmacthomas, 1851–1921. Archives of the Rural District Councils of Lismore, 1899–1925, Waterford, 1899–1925, Dungarvan, 1899–1925, Kilmacthomas, 1899–1921.

Private paper collections including the Lismore Castle papers, 1870–1966; Chearnley papers, 1671–1911; papers relating to Mothel and Carrick-on-Suir; miscellaneous deeds relating to County Waterford.

253 Wesley Historical Society
Irish Branch – Belfast

Address	Edgehill College 9 Lennoxvale Belfast BT9 5BY
Telephone	(02891) 815959
E-mail	archives@irishmethodist.org
Enquiries to	The Honorary Archivist
Opening hours and facilities	9.00–12.30, Mon–Thurs but advisable to make a prior appointment with the Archivist
Guides	Bulletin of the Wesley Historical Society (Irish Branch)

Major collections

Methodist Church in Ireland: Conference reports, agenda and minutes as published, 1878–; Wesleyan Conference minutes, 1752–1878; Primitive Wesleyan Methodist Conference, 1818–78.

Methodist periodicals: *The Methodist Magazine* (Irish edition), 1801–22 (monthly with portraits of Irish preachers); *The Primitive Wesleyan Methodist Magazine*, 1823–78 (bi-monthly); *The Irish Evangelist*, 1859–83 (monthly); *Christian Advocate*, 1823–1923 (weekly); *Irish Christian Advocate*, 1923–71 (weekly); *Methodist Newsletter*, 1973– (monthly).

Minutes and records of the Methodist Women's Organization and the Methodist Missionary Society (Irish Branch).

Selected registers of Irish Methodist circuits.

Microfilms of Methodist registers of Northern Ireland circuits.

Miscellaneous: writings of Methodists (correspondence, diaries, scrapbooks), photographs and other illustrative material, late 18th–21st century.

254 Wesley Historical Society
Ireland Branch – Dublin

Address	Christ Church Sandymount Green Dublin 4
Telephone	(01) 280 7141 (Revd D.A.L. Cooney) (01) 497 2489 (Mr S.C. ffeary-Smyrl)

Enquiries to	As above
Opening hours and facilities	By appointment only

Major collections
Records from various circuits and chapels within the Dublin District of the Methodist Church in Ireland.
Small collections donated by individuals.

255 Westmeath County Library

Address	County Library Headquarters Dublin Road Mullingar County Westmeath
Telephone	(044) 40781/2/3
Fax	(044) 41322
Enquiries to	The County Librarian/ Local Authority Archivist
Opening hours and facilities	9.30–1.00; 2.00–5.00, Mon–Fri
Guides	Marian Keaney, *Westmeath local studies: a guide to sources* (Mullingar, Longford/Westmeath Joint Library Committee, 1981).

Major collections
Grand Jury: presentment books, 1842–99.
Board of Guardian material: Athlone Union, minute books, 1849–1920; abstract of guardians accounts, 1905–21; financial and statistical minute book, 1907–08. Mullingar Union, minute books, 1857–1921; daily diet book, 1857–58; cream account book, 1867–68; general ledgers, 1909–23.
Rural District Council minute books: Athlone No. 1 RDC minute books, 1899–1925; ledgers, 1915–25; rate books, 1923–45. Coole RDC minute books, 1899–1925; loans expenditure book, 1908–16; general ledgers, 1919–25; rate books, 1923–45. Mullingar RDC minute books, 1899–1925; waterworks committee minute book, 1905–22; rate books, 1905–45; personal ledger, 1907–25. Ballymore RDC minute books,

1900–25; register of separate charges, 1904–24; general ledgers, 1905–25; seed and manure supply scheme collection account books, 1918; rate books, 1922–45. Kilbeggan RDC minute books, 1914–17. Delvin RDC minute books, 1919–23; general ledger, 1923–25; rate books, 1923–45.

Board of Health records: county board of health and public assistance (County Home and Hospitals) minute books, 1921–42; contractor's ledger, 1934–43; medical assistance register, Athlone dispensary district, 1935–55; public assistance ledger, 1943–46.

County Council material: valuation lists, 1878–1972; registers of mortgages, 1880–1954; financial records, 1899–1967; minute books, 1899–1988; roads committee minute book, 1912–26; county surveyor's statement of expenditure on works, 1912–32; tuberculosis committee financial statement receipt book, 1918–20; housing maintenance ledger, 1922–28; labourers cottages rent collection books, 1923–71; register of motor cars, 1925–57; tuberculosis advisory committee minute book, 1926–34; attendance register, 1926–35; salary registers, 1927–40; storekeeper's stock book, 1928–43; sewerage, waterworks and burial board minute book, 1928–40; register of driving licences, 1932–75; manager's orders, 1942–77; registers of purchaser's cottages, 1944–56; manager's orders, joint library committee, 1945–88; engineering files, 1948–56; home assistance and expenditure books, 1949–68; grant reconstruction books, 1952–78; rent collection books, 1970–81;

Urban District Council minute books: Athlone UDC minute books, 1901–49; factories and workshops register, 1908–36; registers of cowkeepers and dairymen, 1908–70; rate books, 1911–76; artisans' dwellings rent collection books, 1913–66; poor rate book, 1914; waterworks and sanitary committee minute book, 1914–37; housing minute books, 1923–40; letter books, 1924–37; financial minute books, 1930–37; valuation lists, 1930–52; sanitary officer's report book, 1931–39; housing ledgers, 1933–59; financial statement books, 1933–78; postage book, 1939–48; manager's orders, 1942–60; ledgers of public slaughter houses, 1949–65; combined stock record books, 1949–72; water rent book, 1951–80; waterworks manager's log book, 1958–67.

Town Commissioners: Mullingar Town Commissioners minute books, 1923–57; financial statement records, 1930–73; artisan's dwellings general rentals, 1933–70; rate books, 1937–46; artisan's dwellings rent collection books, 1958–70; postage book, 1960–77.

Trustees of River Deel Drainage Board: minute book, 1869–1945; maintenance rate book, 1923–34.

Upper Inny Drainage Committee: minute book, 1932–40.

Small collection of private material including various rent books, 1816–1924; Athlone Loan Fund Society, 1865–1948.

Sources for local studies including material relating to Westmeath families and writers including Brinsley McNamara, Pakenham family, Fr Paul Walsh, Olive Sharkey, Padraic O'Farrell and Leo Daly. Howard-Bury and Belvedere House Collections, 1800–1940s, from Colonel C.K. Howard-Bury, leader of the first Everest Expedition, and Rex B. Beaumont, Belvedere House, Mullingar.

John Broderick Collection consisting of the novelist's library with inscribed copies of the works of leading Irish and French writers, together with a small collection of literary correspondence.

John Charles Lyons of Ledeston printing press and items of major Westmeath interest printed on it.

Estate papers and maps: Westmeath County Infirmary minute books; collections of photographs, newscuttings.

John B. Burgess Collection, 1885–1960, containing Athlone directories, wills and deeds, church registers, and other printed matter of Athlone interest.

256   Wexford Borough Council

Address	Municipal Buildings Wexford
Telephone	(053) 42611
Fax	(053) 45947
E-mail	postmaster@wexfordboroughcoouncil.ie
Website address	www.wexfordcorp.ie
Enquiries to	The Town Clerk
Opening hours and facilities	9.00–1.00, 2.00–5.00, Mon–Fri; photocopying

Major collections

Minutes of Wexford Corporation, 1776–.

Copies of title documents, 17th century–.

'Lacey Book' and map: record of Corporate Estate by Thomas Lacey, borough treasurer, 1854.

Charter, 1846.

257 Wexford County Archives

Address	Wexford Library Headquarters
	Ardcavan
	Wexford
Telephone	(053) 24922
Fax	(053) 21097
E-mail	libraryhq@wexfordcoco.ie
Enquiries to	The Archivist
Opening hours and facilities	By appointment only; photocopying; photography

Major collections

Board of Guardian records: Wexford Union, 1840–1922; Enniscorthy Union, 1840–1922; Gorey Union, 1840–1919; New Ross Union, 1847–1922.

Grand Jury material, 1858–1900.

Rural District Council records for Wexford, Enniscorthy, Gorey and New Ross, 1899–1925.

Board of Health minute books, 1921–42.

Wexford County Council archives, 1899–1970.

Wexford Harbour Commissioners records: transactions relating to registered ships, 1830–80; arrivals and departures from Wexford Harbour, 1831–1922; minute books, 1857–1960, accounts, 1875–99, record of rocket life-saving apparatus and store, 1900–10; pilot boat diaries, 1930–61.

Courtown Harbour: records of arrivals, shipping and departure of cargo, 1839–65.

County Wexford Infirmary records, 1845–1923.

Trustees of Wexford Free Bridge, 1857–72.

Tate School, Wexford, archives: account book, 1863–88, minute book, 1863–1904; accounts of Governor of school, 1896–1911.

Minute book of Primrose League, Ardcandrisk Habitation,, no. 1084, 1866–96.

Specifications, bill of quantities and form of tender for the erection of six cottages for the Royal National Life Boat Institution, Rosslare station, 1926.

Large collection of estate papers, photographs and family archives, early 16th–late 19th century.

258   Wexford County Museum

Address	Castle Hill Enniscorthy Wexford
Telephone	(054) 35926
Fax	(054) 35926
E-mail	wexmus@iol.ie
Enquiries to	The Honorary Secretary
Opening hours and facilities	10.00–6.00, June–Oct; 2.00–5.30, Feb–May

Major collections
Letters, maps, deeds, miscellaneous papers referring mostly to the 1798 and 1916 rebellions in County Wexford.

259   Wexford Opera Festival

Address	Theatre Royal High Street Wexford
Telephone	(053) 22400
Fax	(053) 24289
E-mail	info@wexfordopera.com
Enquiries to	The Chief Executive Officer
Opening hours and facilities	By appointment

Major collections
Archives of the Wexford Festival from its inception in 1951, documenting festival and theatre development, artistic administration, finance, development of the Festival Council, fringe and associated events. Original material includes artists' biographies, directors' files, correspondence, contracts, minutes, scores, librettos, photographs, scrapbooks, programmes and publicity material

260   Wicklow County Library

Address   UDC Offices
                     Boghall Road
                     Bray
                     County Wicklow

Telephone   (0404) 61732

Enquiries to   The Archivist

Opening hours   By appointment only; photocopying
and facilities

Major collections
Grand Jury presentments; Wicklow County Council minutes; Board of
Guardians minutes, 19th century; Bray Urban District Council minutes;
Rural District Council minutes of Shillelagh and Rathdrum; Wicklow
Board of Health and Public Assistance minutes; Wicklow Urban
District Council minutes; Poor Law Union minutes for Shillelagh and
Rathdrum.

261   Wicklow Port Company

Address   North Quay
                     Wicklow

Telephone   (0404) 67455

Fax   (0404) 67455

Enquiries to   The Secretary/Harbour Master

Opening hours   9.00–1.00, 2.00–5.00, Mon–Fri
and facilities

Major collections
Minute books, 1897–1954; damp press letter books, 1908–27; harbour dues
and tolls, 1891–1965; account books, receipt books and pay orders,
1854–1970; correspondence, deeds, leases, maps and drawings.

262 Wilson's Hospital School

Address	Multyfarnham County Westmeath
Telephone	(044) 71115
Fax	(044) 71563
E-mail	WILSONSH@iol.ie
Website address	www.whs.ie
Enquiries to	The Bursar
Opening hours and facilities	By appointment; photocopying

Major collections

Registers of old men and boys, 1761–1923; registers of pupils, 1923–45, roll books, 1886–.

National School records: roll books, 1898–1946; daily report books, 1898–1938.

Weekly accounts, 1836–9, 1842–5, 1848–52, 1857–63, 1943–9, 1966–74; Wardens' accounts, 1895–1967.

Minutes of the Trustees and Guardians, 1913–16

Appendices

1. Archives at present closed

The following organisations, some of which supplied entries for a previous edition of this directory, have indicated that they hold archives but are unable at the present time to provide access of any sort to their holdings.

Adelaide & Meath Hospital Dublin
Augustinian House of Studies, Ballyboden, Dublin 16
Carmelite Order, Ballinteer, Dublin 16
Cork & Ross Diocesan Archives
Daughters of Charity of St Vincent de Paul, Blackrock, County Dublin
Ferns Diocesan Archives
Kildare County Archives
National Womens' Council of Ireland
St John of God Sisters, Wexford
Strokestown Park House, County Roscommon
University of Limerick Archives

2. Archives transferred

The following organisations provided entries for previous editions of this *Directory*. The custody of their archives or responsibility for their functions has since been transferred to the institutions indicated.

Armagh Diocesan Archives: Cardinal Tomás Ó Fiaich Library & Archive
Bantry House: National University of Ireland, Cork, Boole Library
Castletown House: in the temporary custody of the Irish Architectural Archive
Carlow County Heritage Society: Carlow Central Library
Down & Dromore and Connor Diocesan Library: Public Record Office of Northern Ireland
Dundalk Harbour Commissioners: Louth County Archives
Fianna Fáil: University College Dublin Archives Department
Meath Diocesan Registry: Representative Church Body Library, Dublin

Office of Public Works: National Archives
Ordnance Survey: National Archives
Public Record Office of Ireland: National Archives
Royal Zoological Society of Ireland: Trinity College Library Dublin,
    Manuscripts Department
St Canice's Cathedral Library, Kilkenny: Representative Church Body
    Library, Dublin
St Patrick's Cathedral, Dublin: Representative Church Body Library, Dublin
State Paper Office: National Archives
University College Dublin College Archives Service: University College
    Dublin Archives Department

3. Related organisations and institutions

Association of Church Archivists of Ireland

Honorary Secretary: Sr Marie Bernadette O'Leary
                         Religious Sisters of Charity
                         Caritas
                         15 Guilford Road
                         Sandymount
                         Dublin 4

Telephone: (01) 269 7833
Fax: (01) 260 3085

Founded in 1980 as the Association of Religious Archivists of Ireland; present title adopted in 1992; holds regular meetings; organises occasional short training courses and workshops; membership open to anyone involved with religious archives of any denomination.

Association of Professional Genealogists in Ireland

                         c/o Genealogical Office
                         2 Kildare Street
                         Dublin 2

Fax: (01) 662 1062
E-mail: apgi@dublin.com
Website   http://indigo.ie/~apgi

Acts as a regulating body to maintain standards among its members and protect the interests of clients. Members bound by the APGI code of practice, undertake fee-paid genealogical research. Brochure and list of members available.

Irish Manuscripts Commission

Chairman   Professor Geoffrey Hand
                        73 Merrion Square
                        Dublin 2

Telephone: (01) 676 1610
E-mail: irmss@eircom.net

Established in 1928 to report on and publish significant manuscript material; publishes the journal *Analecta Hibernica;* members appointed by the Minister for Arts, Sport and Tourism.

Irish Society for Archives

Chairman   Dr R. Refaussé
Honorary Secretary: Ms Ursula Mitchell
                        Manuscripts Department
                        Trinity College Dublin Library
                        Dublin 2

E-mail: umitchell@tcd.ie
Website   www.ucd.ie/~archives

General interest organisation founded in 1970 to promote awareness on all matters relating to archives in Ireland; organises a lecture series and publishes the journal *Irish Archives*; membership open to all.

National Archives Advisory Council

                        73 Merrion Square
                        Dublin 2.
Chairman   Judge Bryan McMahon
Secretary   Pat Corcoran
                        Room 336
                        Frederick Buildings
                        Sth Frederick St.
                        Dublin 2

E-mail: patcorcoran@dast.gov.ie

Established under the provisions of the *National Archives Act 1986*, to advise the Taoiseach in the exercise of his powers under the Act and on all matters affecting archives and their use by the public; the Taoiseach's powers are now devolved to the Minister for Arts, Sport and Tourism to whom the Council submits an annual report which is laid before the Houses of the Oireachtas; twelve members appointed by the Minister.

Society of Archivists, Ireland

Honorary Secretary: Clare Hackett
Guinness Archive, Diageo Ireland
Guinness Storehouse
St James's Gate
Dublin 8

Telephone: (01) 471 4557
E-mail: clare.hackett@guinnessudv.com

The professional body in the United Kingdom and Ireland for archivists, records managers and conservators; organised on a regional basis with special interest groups drawn from the total membership; represents the interests of the profession, sets professional standards, monitors and recognises training courses, and maintains a professional register; meetings held regularly at regional and national level; SoA, Ireland has published *Standards for the development of archives services in Ireland* (1997); Society publishes the *Journal of the Society of Archivists* and a series of *Best practice guidelines*.

University College Dublin Archives Department

University College Dublin
Belfield
Dublin 4

Telephone: (01) 716 7545
Fax: (01) 716 1146
E-mail: Ailsa.Holland@ucd.ie
Website: www.ucd.ie/~archives

Provides a one-year, full-time postgraduate Higher Diploma in Archival Studies (HDipAS), a professional qualification recognised by the Society of Archivists; course details available on the website; detailed prospectus available from the department.

Index

The numbers refer to the Directory number.

The numbers in this index are the Directory numbers.

Index

Christ's Hospital, London, 60
Christian Brothers, 5, 89, 90
Church of Ireland College of Education Archives, 21
Church of Ireland Training College collection, 21
Church of Ireland, 15, 192
Church Temporalities Commission, 96
Cistercian Order, 152, 153
City Factory, Derry, 39
Civics Institute of Ireland, 51
Clancy, Canon John, 113
Clancy, John, bishop of Elphin, 58
Clare County Council, 22
Clare County Library, Local Studies Centre, 23
Clarendon Street Church, 41
Clarke, Harry, 82
Claytons Woollen Mills, Navan, 139
Clements estate papers, Counties Leitrim and Donegal, 159
Clifden–Galway railway, 167
Clogher Diocesan Archives, 24
Clogher Diocesan Archives, Church of Ireland, 25
Cloghran stud farm, 63
Clohessy, Fr, 210
Clonalis House, 26
Clonbrock collection, 161
Clonbrock estate papers, County Galway, 159
Cloncurry papers, 76
Clonfert Diocesan Archives, 27
Clongowes Wood College, 28
Clover Meats, Waterford, 112
Cloyne Diocesan Archives, 29
Cobbe family, 170
Cochrane, Captain Ernest, 44
Coghlan, Brian, 200
Coláiste Íde Preparatory School, Dingle, 142
Coleraine, 99
Colgan, N., 156
Colles, Abraham, 196
Collins papers, 145
Collins, Michael, 242
Collon estate papers, 133
Committee on Ulster Folklife and Traditions, 238
Communication Workers' Union, 95
Communications Union of Ireland, 95
Communist Party of Ireland, 30
Companies Registration Office, 31
Company of Apothecaries Hall, 6
Company of Goldsmiths, 77
Congested Districts Board, 96
Congregation de Propaganda Fide in Rome, 113

Congregation of Dominican Sisters, Cabra, 43
Congregation of the Mission, Irish Province, 250
Congregation of the Most Holy Redeemer, 188
Congregation of the Religious of Jesus and Mary, 103
Conroy, George, 7
Conry, Roisin, 164
Contemporary Music Centre Ireland, 32
Conyngham estate papers, 159
Cooke, Eddie, 101
Cooke, Robert, 18
Cookstown District Council, 231
Coolatin estate papers, County Wicklow, 159
Cooper Penrose estate, 34
Cooper family, County Tipperary, 234
Coopers' Guild of Dublin, 79
Coote papers, 128
Coppinger estate, 34
Córas Iompair Éireann, 33, 98
Corcoran SJ, Timothy, 242
Cork & Ross Diocesan Archives, & p. 199
Cork Archives Institute, 34
Cork Butter Market, 34
Cork Coopers' Society, 34
Cork Distillers, 34
Cork District Model School, 34
Cork Grafton Club, 34
Cork Harbour Commissioners, 35
Cork Plumbers' Union, 34
Cork Presbyterian Congregation at Princes Street, 34
Cork Public Museum, 36
Cork School of Art library, 37
Cork Sick Poor Society, 34
Cork Steam Ship Company, 34
Cork Theatre Company, 101
Cork Theatre, 34
Cork Typographical Union, 34
Cork Workers' Council, 34
Corkery, Daniel, 166
Corrigan, Sir Dominick, 195
Cosgrave, Ephraim MacDowel, 200
Costello, John A., 242
Courtenay estate, 34
Courtown Harbour, 257
Cow Pock Institution, 195
Cox, Arthur, 242
Coyle, Kathleen, 39
Coyne, Bernard, bishop of Elphin, 58
Craig, Maurice, 87
Craigavon Arts Committee, 231
Craigavon District Council, 231
Crawford Municipal Art Gallery, 37

The numbers in this index are the Directory numbers.

205

The numbers in this index are the Directory numbers.

The numbers in this index are the Directory numbers.

The numbers in this index are the Directory numbers.

Index

The numbers in this index are the Directory numbers.

The numbers in this index are the Directory numbers.

The numbers in this index are the Directory numbers.

The numbers in this index are the Directory numbers.

The numbers in this index are the Directory numbers.

The numbers in this index are the Directory numbers.

The numbers in this index are the Directory numbers.

The numbers in this index are the Directory numbers.

Index

The numbers in this index are the Directory numbers.